A Romance on Three Legs

A Romance
on
Three Legs

Glenn Gould's Obsessive Quest for the Perfect Piano

Katie Hafner

BLOOMSBURY

Frontispiece: In April 1957, Gould tried out various Steinways at the Columbia Recording Studio on Thirtieth Street in Manhattan. This was Gould's first session with photographer Don Hunstein, who would photograph him many times over the years. Photograph by Don Hunstein, courtesy of Sony BMG Music Entertainment.

Published by Bloomsbury USA, New York
Distributed to the trade by Macmillan

All papers used by Bloomsbury USA are natural, recyclable products made from wood grown in well-managed forests. The manufacturing processes conform to the environmental regulations of the country of origin.

LIBRARY OF CONGRESS CATALOGING-IN-PUBLICATION DATA

Hafner, Katie.
A romance on three legs : Glenn Gould's obsessive quest for the perfect piano / Katie Hafner.
p. cm.
ISBN-13: 978-1-59691-524-4
ISBN-10: 1-59691-524-2
1. Gould, Glenn—Criticism and interpretation.   2. Steinway & Sons—History.   3. Steinway Piano—History.   4. Piano—Construction—United States.   I. Title.

ML417.G68H28 2008
786.2092—dc22
2007048808

First U.S. Edition 2008

10 9 8 7 6 5 4 3 2 1

Designed by Rachel Reiss
Typeset by Westchester Book Group
Printed in the United States of America by Quebecor World Fairfield

For Brad, who saw me through.

And for my mother, cheerleader extraordinaire.

Contents

Ottawa, 1983

IT ARRIVED IN A LARGE moving van: 226 cartons filled with objects that, had they belonged to anyone else, could just as easily have been destined for a landfill. Each box contained thousands of loose sheets of yellow-lined paper covered with a nearly indecipherable scrawl in black felt-tip pen. And scores of the pens themselves.

The boxes also contained hundreds of cassette tapes, hotel-room and rental-car keys by the dozen, a deck of playing cards, two wristwatches, a collection of porcelain dogs (mostly collies), a number of stray cuff links and leather wallets, three conductor's batons, one mug inscribed DON'T SHOOT THE PIANO PLAYER, photographs, radio scripts, canceled checks, badly frayed shirts and trousers, two pairs of beige woolen gloves without fingertips, gray woolen cardigans, a pile of undershirts, two tweed caps, and countless bottles filled with prescription drugs: pills for blood pressure, colds, joint pain, insomnia, and circulation.

There was also a large box that had been shipped by Steinway & Sons years earlier; it was filled with a complete set of piano hammers. Inside the drawer of a small table that was part of this ragtag collection were twelve wooden blocks that were used for raising the height of various pianos.

But the most famous artifact that arrived in the van was the "pygmy chair," a battered, stout, unusually low wooden folding chair that was held together with brackets, glue, and piano wire. The chair had once had a padded seat, but that was now long gone. The only way a person could keep from falling through it while seated was to perch on a lone wooden support that ran from front to back.

These were the collected belongings of Glenn Gould, the brilliant and eccentric Canadian pianist, one of the country's leading cultural treasures, who had died in 1982 at the age of fifty. His abbreviated life had been punctuated by idiosyncrasies unusual even for a classical musician. After a brief but meteoric concert career, in 1964, at the age of thirty-one, he had renounced public life, confined himself to his native Toronto, and dedicated himself to the recording studio. His particular achievements in playing the works of J. S. Bach as well as certain lesser-known composers of twentieth-century music, along with his odd personality, had captured worldwide attention—and passionate fans.

Gould's playing evoked a visceral response from people who had never thought to stop and really listen to classical music. There was something about the silence between and behind each note, the richness of the different voices, that captured the imagination and caused listeners to feel that their lives had been deepened and enhanced. Thousands of people over the years had heard Gould's best-selling 1955 recording of Bach's Goldberg Variations—the little air and its thirty virtuosic variations—and became lifelong fans.

For some, including people who knew the music well, Gould's playing enabled them to hear new things. Others, including those who had no special affinity for classical music, reported feeling an intuitive connection to the music when they first heard Gould playing. Bruno Monsaingeon, a French filmmaker and violinist, was in a record store in Moscow in the late

1960s when he chanced upon a couple of recordings by Gould, whose playing was unfamiliar to him. When the filmmaker listened to the records, he likened the experience to a religious epiphany, as if a voice were saying, "Follow me." Monsaingeon would devote the next two decades of his life to making films about Gould. A heart surgeon in London encouraged every patient to listen to Gould's recordings of Bach before he operated. A UPS driver in Roanoke, Virginia, told a Gould scholar about the moment when a few phrases of the Goldberg Variations came over the truck's radio station and she instinctively began to reach for the dial to change to a different station. But she was turning a corner and needed both hands on the wheel, so the music continued. And continued—transforming her into a lifelong devotee of Gould's work.

Gould's sudden death from a stroke was one that no one, least of all Gould, had had time to prepare for. Once the decision was made by his lawyer to send all of his possessions to the National Library of Canada in Ottawa, the task of sorting through everything fell to a library-staff member and an outside music expert who was hired to help. Having disposed of the impersonal objects—telephone books, take-out pizza menus—they worked their way through the mountain of personal miscellany and began to feel that throwing *anything* away would be sacrilegious, in part because the great Gould himself had been unable to part with it. So they sent every last scrap of yellow-lined paper, every Christmas card and bottle of aspirin, to Ottawa, to the National Library, the country's repository of national treasures.

Curators and musicologists would spend the next several years sorting through the papers and the music, eventually transferring much of it to microfilm to save the originals from being handled by biographers and curiosity seekers. Some of the artifacts, such as clothing, wallets, figurines, and keys, were eventually sent to the Canadian Museum of Civilization, just across the Ottawa River in Gatineau, Quebec. After a few years the curators placed the pygmy chair, the only form of seating that Gould would use while playing the piano, in a glass display case, where it assumed a ghostly presence next to the elevators on the archive's fourth floor.

And then there was the piano, which the National Library had decided to purchase from Gould's estate. An eight-foot-eleven-and-one-quarter-inch Steinway concert grand, it was known as CD 318 (*C* to signify its special status as having been put aside for the use of Steinway concert artists, and *D* denoting it as the largest of Steinway's pianos). Like every Steinway piano, it bore its own serial number: 317194. Helmut Kallmann, the head of the library's music division, oversaw the delivery of CD 318 and later described how all 1,325 pounds of it were unloaded by three expert burly movers and unceremoniously deposited in the ground-floor lobby of the library. They untied the straps, removed the pads, attached the legs, requested a signature, and left.

A musician himself, Kallmann was a devotee of Gould's work. In the 1960s, he had occasionally crossed paths with Gould at the Canadian Broadcasting Corporation, where Kallmann supervised the music library. Gould showed up from time to time to pick up musical scores and often stopped to chat. The pianist's eccentricities were always evident, as was his charm. Gould once endeared himself to Kallmann by asking, "What key do you think my personality is in?"

Like most Gould fans, Kallmann was familiar with the pianist's legendary Chickering, a one-hundred-year-old small grand that Gould had famously adored. But when it came time to purchase one of Gould's pianos for the National Library's permanent collection, Kallmann and his colleagues in the music division knew it had to be CD 318, the piano that had seen Gould through nearly every recording of his career.

Steinway had made many beautiful instruments over the years—not just the classic ebonized concert grands, but also a number of art-case pianos. Among the best-known are an elaborate white-and-gilt decorative piano made for Cornelius Vanderbilt, with paintings of Apollo surrounded by cherubs, and a piano created for the White House, with legs formed of carved eagles. For the Waldorf-Astoria Hotel in New York, Steinway had built a tortoiseshell decoration surmounted by a candelabrum. For the oil magnate E. L. Doheny, the company designed a gilded piano in a Louis XV style with carved legs and elaborate moldings. Even Steinway's standard-issue polished-ebony concert grands were stately and handsome, if also austere.

Not so this instrument.

The piano that arrived in the early afternoon at the loading bay behind the library, its black case scratched and dented, the lid slightly out of alignment and disfigured by visible gouges, looked every bit the orphan. The archivists in Ottawa knew that this tired-looking instrument had been Gould's favorite concert grand. And they knew that there had once been an accident that had for a time rendered the piano all but unplayable. But that was all they knew.

One evening shortly after the piano's arrival, after everyone else had left for the day and he was sure he was alone, Kallmann sat down at CD 318 and played on it a bit. He was first taken aback, and then impressed, by the instrument's extreme responsiveness, its improbably light touch. No wonder Gould, whose musicianship was so closely tied to his dexterity, had been so attached to it. Kallmann suddenly felt as if he understood something crucial about the great pianist and the piano he had loved. During Gould's lifetime, fans had speculated that the piano he used must have been altered in some extraordinary way, perhaps rigged with special equipment that would make it possible for Gould's fingers to fly as fast as they did. But Kallmann closely examined the instrument and found nothing out of the ordinary, no piano equivalent of a warp drive. Using ordinary tuning and regulating tools, a piano technician had managed to give the piano its hair-trigger action. Kallmann marveled: That must have been some technician.

Kallmann took it upon himself to investigate CD 318's provenance. One of the first telephone calls he placed was to the T. Eaton Company, the large Toronto department store whose piano department had been responsible for the instrument for nearly three decades before Gould had purchased it in 1973. Kallmann was directed to Muriel Mussen, who had recently retired from Eaton's after more than thirty years working in the piano department, where she was in charge of choosing from among a stable of large grands for visiting concert artists.

Oh, yes, said Mussen when Kallmann explained why he was calling. CD 318. And Glenn Gould. Of course. The piano, she said, had come to Eaton's around 1946, and for years famous pianists who came through Toronto in the course of a concert tour had played on it. But as the piano had aged, it had lost its appeal. In fact, in the 1950s, concert pianists began to complain about it. And in 1960, just as Eaton's was preparing to dispose of it—by which she meant that the company planned to ship it back to Steinway in exchange for a newer instrument—Glenn Gould chanced upon it.

From the moment he lifted the fallboard, Gould was smitten. He had been famously fussy about his pianos and spent years rejecting most factory-issue Steinways. But here was a piano whose qualities just happened to be ideally aligned to his particular style of playing. Before long, he was playing on CD 318 exclusively. That piano, Mussen observed, came to be as eccentric as Glenn Gould himself, coddled and tweaked and regulated by Mr. Gould's principal technician—a man Muriel Mussen referred to simply as Verne—to achieve the supremely responsive keyboard action that Gould required. She explained that Gould grew so attached to CD 318, and became so fearful of unfamiliar pianos, that he insisted on taking it with him for important concerts. Later, after he stopped performing in public, he made nearly all his recordings on CD 318.

Once, Mussen recalled, in the course of extolling the virtues of this piano, Gould told her something about his relationship to CD 318 that she would never forget: "This is the first time in history," he said, "that there has ever been a romance on three legs."

ONE

Toronto

*Sixteen-year-old Glenn and his English
setter Nick at the keyboard. This
photograph accompanied a profile that ran
in the* Evening Telegram *in February
1949.* Photographer unknown, courtesy
of the Library and Archives Canada and
the Glenn Gould Estate.

Glenn Gould was born in 1932 to a solidly middle-class family in a leafy, peaceful neighborhood on the eastern edge of Toronto.

Glenn's father, Bert, was a furrier who had played the violin in his youth; Glenn's mother, Florence, was a pianist and music teacher. Both were singers. The two-story brick house where Glenn would live more than half his life was unostentatious, but the family was affluent enough to buy cars and radios and to afford live-in housekeepers and a nanny, and the Goulds' relative prosperity kept them largely shielded from the Depression.

The Goulds—Methodists on one side, Presbyterians on the other—were quietly pious people. Both Bert and Florence had come out of traditions that stressed morality and the authority of the Bible, valued reason over passion, and considered idleness a sin. They were devout churchgoers, and throughout his childhood Glenn accompanied his parents to Sunday services.

A life of music was preordained for Glenn. Florence was convinced of her son's musical genius even when he was an infant. "She was very determined he was going to be a musician," Glenn's cousin Jessie Greig recalled years later. As a small child, Glenn was verbally expressive and spoke full sentences before he was a year old. But music was the realm where he was to find true expression. When Glenn was three, his mother noticed that he could correctly name a note being sung on a record, a sign of perfect pitch, the psychoacoustical ability that enables a person to recognize the pitch of every note, to know how a C sounds the way most people recognize the color blue. Fascinated by her son's acuity, Florence invented a game in which she would sit at the piano and Glenn would remain in a distant room in the house. Florence would play a chord on the piano and Glenn would call out the full name. He could do this not just with simple triads, but also with complicated chords involving more than the usual number of tones. His father once noted that when something happened that would normally cause a child to cry—if he fell down, for example—young Glenn would hum instead.

He was inordinately sensitive as a small child. Not only did he have a tactile hypersensitivity both in touching and being touched, but he disliked bright colors. His favorite colors, he often said, were "battleship gray and midnight blue." Throughout his life, he could not think clearly in a room painted in primary colors. When his parents took him to see Walt Disney's *Fantasia,* the "awful riot of color" gave him a headache and left him feeling nauseated.

Glenn was also a very aural child. His senses of sight and taste and smell were not well developed, but musical sound could move him deeply. Unlike most small children, Glenn did not need to bang on a piano's keys in order to be interested in what he was hearing. As soon as he was old enough to be held on his grandmother's knee at the piano, he would press the keys one by one with what were already long, tapered fingers, holding a key down until the sound had faded completely, fascinated by its diminishment.

At three, before he could read words, Glenn could read music. A childhood nanny recalled that this extraordinary ability led Florence to suggest that her son might be the reincarnation of one of the great composers. Gould himself once said he had never been pushed to learn music or to play the piano, but took to it as if he had fallen into a swimming pool and become an avid swimmer as a result. And his agile hands were an asset he guarded instinctively, even as a small child. If someone threw, or even rolled, a ball at him, he pulled his hands away or turned his back. "It was as if he knew he had to protect those fingers for some reason," his father said years later.

By the time Glenn was four, his fascination with the piano had evolved into formal lessons with Florence, thus further cementing an already strong bond between mother and son, and it was in those lessons that Glenn's gift became even more apparent. To reinforce her son's innate musical talent, Florence, who was also a voice instructor, taught Glenn to sing along to everything he played, planting the seeds for what would become a lifelong habit. Florence was an exacting teacher. "He was never allowed to play a wrong note," recalled Glenn's cousin Jessie. "If he did, she stopped immediately right there and then."

The piano became the place where Glenn preferred to spend his time. Far from having to force their child to practice, the Goulds had the opposite problem. When they needed to discipline him, they shut the piano down and locked the fallboard, a measure his father described as "far worse than any corporal punishment."

Even before his teens, Glenn had decided on a career as a concert pianist. In 1938, his parents took him to the Toronto Symphony. The concert, especially the full sound of the entire orchestra, made a deep impression on the young man, who later told an interviewer that he remembered being brought home afterward in the car. "I was falling asleep—and I was in that wonderful state of half awakeness in which you hear all sorts of incredible sounds going through your mind, and they were all orchestral sounds. But I was playing them all."

Elizabeth Fox, a friend and frequent visitor to the Gould household, once compared the threesome—Bert, Florence, and their very unusual son—to the family in E. B. White's *Stuart Little*, in which a human couple's child is a mouse, a sweet little guy who also happens to be freakishly different. "When you were at the Goulds' house, you'd think, these people have produced something that is not of them," she said. "He's dressed . . . like a human being, and he plays the piano, but they were constantly in awe."

Unlike many parents of talented children, Florence and Bert had no desire to push Glenn onto the concert stage, preferring to let him develop at his own pace. When he was five he was allowed to play the piano in public for the first time, at a Sunday-afternoon church service, where he accompanied his parents as they sang "Revive Us Again," a nineteenth-century hymn. And he performed sporadically thereafter. But for years, and well into Glenn's teens, the Goulds kept their son out of the public sphere, which they intuitively sensed would put a strain on his mental or physical health—or both. And while competitions were the typical route to success and recognition for most young pianists, as he grew older Glenn steered clear of them. Throughout his life Gould would vehemently oppose any sort of musical activity that smacked of competition, claiming that such contests left their participants "victims of a spiritual lobotomy." Still, and not surprisingly, at the few competitions his parents did enter him in, which consisted of three Kiwanis Music Festivals in the mid-1940s, he always walked away with several prizes.

For Glenn's education, his parents started out by engaging a private tutor. But by the time he was eight years old and ready for grade two, they enrolled him at Williamson Road Public School, which bordered the back of the Goulds' property. He passed his grade with such ease he was permitted to skip ahead to grade four. In general, his father recalled, Glenn was a happy, "normal, healthy, fun-loving boy" with a sunny disposition. Robert Fulford, who lived next door, described Glenn as a "lovable" small child. "He was very funny," Fulford said. "He didn't take himself very seriously. He took music very seriously, but not himself." Fulford remembered that when they walked home from school, Glenn sometimes conducted an invisible orchestra, both arms flailing as he hummed the different parts.

But as adolescence set in, Glenn became increasingly lost in a world of music. And the traits that defined him as an adult—hypochondria, obsessive and reclusive tendencies—gradually manifested themselves. He had few friends. It didn't help that he detested group activities, especially sports, and his separateness made him the object of frequent teasing. He once told an interviewer that he wasn't beaten up every day; he was beaten up every other day.

If Glenn related to anything outside of music, it was animals. When he bicycled through the countryside near his parents' lakeside vacation cottage outside of Toronto, he sang to the cows. His pets included rabbits, turtles, a fully functioning skunk, goldfish named Bach, Beethoven, Chopin, and Haydn, and a parakeet named Mozart. There was also a series of beloved dogs: a big Newfoundland named Buddy, an English setter named Sir Nickolson of Garelocheed—or Nick for short—and, later, Banquo, a collie. One of Glenn's childhood dreams was to someday create a preserve for old, injured, and stray animals on Manitoulin Island, north of Toronto, where he wanted to live out his old age by himself, surrounded by animals.

At an early age, Gould established a strong identification with a puritan sensibility. Throughout his adult life he would often say that it was he who was the Last Puritan rather than Oliver Alden, the titular hero of George Santayana's novel, a book he admired greatly. Oliver was a serious, duty-bound young man; his searching, restless mind arrived at many understandings, yet he was unable to live the life of the mind as free play, to take delight in where those understandings might lead him.

Florence Gould was passionately devoted to and extremely protective of her sensitive, gifted son. In the winter, she kept him excessively bundled against the elements—even when it wasn't cold outside. And year-round she warned him against the perils of germs. Her hypercaution laid the foundation for her son's lifelong fear of illness. For his entire life, Gould wrapped himself in woolen scarves, mittens—which he often wore over fingerless gloves—caps, and heavy winter coats, even on the hottest summer days. As he grew older, Gould developed an extensive repertoire of eccentric habits aimed at keeping sickness at bay: He avoided shaking people's hands and insisted on keeping room temperatures at eighty degrees, no matter the season, even if it meant using every available space heater.

As an adult, Gould liked to claim he was largely a self-taught musician. But there was in fact a teacher who made deep and lasting impressions on him. At the age of ten, when he had mastered the first book of Bach's *Well-Tempered Clavier* and was enveloping himself still more cocoonlike in music, his parents enrolled him at the Toronto Conservatory of Music. His mother, aware that his talents had outgrown her, began to seek a teacher more suited to her son's rapidly advancing level.

In 1942, after consulting several people, including Sir Ernest MacMillan, the conservatory's principal, Florence found Alberto Guerrero, who was to be Glenn's only teacher after her. Guerrero, fifty-eight years old when he began teaching Glenn, had enjoyed a childhood even more privileged and focused on music than his new student's. Guerrero was born and raised in Chile. In contrast to the later claims of his most famous pupil, Guerrero was in fact a self-educated pianist, with no time spent in formal study. It is rare for someone who attained such a high degree of professional standing to be genuinely self-taught, but this was indeed the case with Guerrero: He learned *en famille*. His father was a prominent industrialist; his mother was a pianist, and she and Alberto's older brother gave him lessons. By the time he was in his early twenties, he had established himself as a brilliant solo pianist, performing throughout Chile. In 1916 he made his New York debut, and two years later he accepted a teaching job in Toronto at the Hambourg Conservatory, a private music school that had opened a few years earlier. In 1922 he switched to the Toronto Conservatory, where he stayed for the rest of his life.

When young Glenn Gould began studying with Guerrero, it was clear to the teacher that his new pupil was already independent-minded as a musician. Guerrero once said, "The whole secret of teaching Glenn is to let him discover things for himself." Still, Glenn was open to suggestion. Although later in life Gould seldom cited Guerrero (or anyone else, for that matter) as an influence on his playing, signs of Guerrero's nine years of guidance were everywhere. Guerrero shaped Gould's technique and his musical taste, particularly his affinity for early music, especially Bach, whose music Guerrero played in concert far more than other pianists did. Guerrero's love of such music made a lasting impression on his young student, as did his admiration for the atonal works of Arnold Schoenberg.

Guerrero instilled some early habits in Glenn, including a variety of unusual limbering and strengthening exercises. Lessons often began with arm massage. To build strength and dexterity, Guerrero had his students practice squeezing a rubber ball. He also had them rotate the wrist or elbow while keeping the hand loose and play scales as smoothly as possible with just one finger.

Then there was the "tapping" exercise, whose goal was to improve ease and evenness of touch and enhance the clarity and separation of individual notes. As John Beckwith, the author of a biography of Guerrero, has explained it, the tapping consisted of placing the five fingers of one hand on the keys and tapping each of those fingers with the nonplaying hand. The idea was to record in the brain what it was like to play with a minimum of muscle movement, as the fingers alone did the work. This exercise was followed by slow, staccato practice before the piece was brought up to tempo. Glenn became an enthusiastic adopter of the tapping exercise. Wrote Beckwith, "It accounts for the clarity of individual notes in Gould's fast runs, one of his most indelible personal trademarks as a player."

Guerrero instructed his students to study the score away from the piano, and Glenn became especially adept at this. By his late teens he was spending at least half his practice time away from the instrument, poring over musical scores. In years to come, people were astounded to learn that a musician could do so much work in his head, spending relatively little time at the piano, and yet play with such remarkable precision.

Guerrero also encouraged Glenn to think of the piano not just as a percussion instrument, but to hear and experience the ways that it embraced aspects of other instruments: strings, woodwinds, lutes, and harpsichords. Although Glenn didn't use the pedal much in general, he found that, with Guerrero's words in mind, using it on occasion helped get him closer to an orchestral sonority. In an interview he gave much later in his life, he said, "Always in the back of my mind, certainly in my postadolescent period, anyway, there has been a substitute sonority such as orchestra or string quartet, to which I have tried to relate whatever I am doing, rather than approaching the music as keyboard music per se." Gould did this, he said, because he believed that for the great majority of important composers, the piano was a substitute system. "It's been there to allow the performance of music that would otherwise be realized by a string quartet, a concerto grosso ensemble, by a full symphony, whatever."

In 1946, at age fourteen, Gould received his diploma from the conservatory and continued to study with Guerrero. That year marked his first performance with the Toronto Symphony, where he played Beethoven's Fourth Concerto. Reviewers gushed. "How awesome are the ways of genius in a child," wrote the critic for the Toronto *Evening Telegram*. "For Glenn Gould is a genius." The critic for the national paper, the *Toronto Globe and Mail*, marveled at the effect of Glenn's speedy hands. "His is not a heavy tone," she wrote, "but delicacy of phrasing and timing give it clear carrying power."

Glenn remarked years later that the performance was "the one most exciting moment in my entire life." Yet he could recall few specifics about his playing. He did, however, remember the dog hair that Nick had left on his trouser legs when he greeted him before the concert. In trying to pick off the hairs during a couple of lengthy orchestral passages, Glenn got so distracted that he almost lost his place in the finale. "I learned the first valuable lesson of my association with the Toronto Symphony Orchestra," he later said. "Either pay attention or keep short-haired dogs."

From an early age, Gould adopted an unusual and intimately physical relationship with his instrument. Sometimes he lowered his face so close to the keyboard that it looked as if he was playing the piano with his nose. And it often seemed that he was hugging the instrument. He developed a playing style that was largely focused on the tips of his long, nimble fingers, and he liked to sit low—several inches below the place where most pianists sit—with his elbows dangling below the keyboard or flapping out to the sides, often with his wrists well below finger level. It was an odd approach; Gould appeared to be reaching for the keys from below. Guerrero also sat low, as did two other pianists Gould had grown to admire, Rosalyn Tureck and Artur Schnabel. But Gould did so to exaggerated effect. He believed this position allowed him a sense of intimate connection with the keys and more control over the finer nuances of tone, phrasing, dynamics, and the contrapuntal complexities in much early music.

Indeed it was well suited to his particular repertoire. Had he wanted to play a great deal of, say, Chopin and Liszt, such a position would have been untenable, because sitting as he did limited his ability to hit the keys from above with maximum strength. It made it more difficult to bring down the requisite force for a true fortissimo or to really attack the far ends of the keyboard, as is often required in climactic passages in nineteenth-century music. And Gould acknowledged this limitation. "It's difficult for me to get a really big sound, as in some of Liszt's fortissimos," he once said. Yet Gould's "rather hunchbacked" technique gave him "finger clarity, better definition and feeling" for the composers he preferred, especially Bach, whose music required far less horizontal and vertical movement.

When he was fifteen, he began to give concerts as a full-fledged professional pianist and became the frequent subject of profiles in Canadian newspapers and magazines. But he was in no rush to expand his performing schedule or to increase his fame, and for several years he confined his appearances to Canada. Finally, in early 1955, at the age of twenty-two, he went to the United States, where he made his debut in Washington, D.C., playing an unconventional assortment of music including Webern's Variations, Orlando Gibbons's Lord of Salisbury Pavan, and the Bach Partita in G Major. A week later he repeated the same program at Town Hall in New York, before an audience that included some prominent pianists who had been hearing about the delicate and gangly pianist with the unorthodox style and wanted to see Glenn Gould for themselves. Gary Graffman and Eugene Istomin, both rising stars, were astonished to hear what Graffman described later as a fully developed original. "He had a hand in his pocket as he walked out," said Graffman. "And as soon as he started to play, I just listened to the music and was absolutely floored."

The critics, too, were taken with the performance. "This

young pianist is clearly a dedicated, sensitive poet of the keyboard," wrote the critic for the New York *Herald-Tribune*. And John Briggs, a reviewer for the *Times*, said Gould "left no doubt of his powers as a technician." Although the review was short, it captured an essential reason for Gould's ability to mesmerize an audience: "The most rewarding aspect of Mr. Gould's playing . . . is that technique as such is in the background. The impression that is uppermost is not one of virtuosity but of expressiveness. One is able to hear the music."

After the concert, Graffman and a few other young pianists were introduced to him at a party in his honor. Graffman noticed that Gould drank only milk and excused himself several times to wash his hands.

As it happened, David Oppenheim, the director of Columbia Records' Masterworks division, was in the audience that night. Oppenheim had gone to the recital because he had heard from a friend that the young Gould might be another Dinu Lipatti, the Romanian pianist who was known for his perfect finger control and purity of sound. Lipatti had died of cancer a few years earlier, at age thirty-three, leaving behind a legion of grief-stricken admirers. At Town Hall Oppenheim was not disappointed. He was so taken with the sheer originality of Gould's playing that he immediately offered him an exclusive contract. When he asked Gould what he wanted to play for his first recording, Gould replied that he wanted to perform Bach's Goldberg Variations. Surprised, Oppenheim suggested Gould consider a different work of Bach's—perhaps the Inventions. There were many reasons for Oppenheim's objection. The Goldberg Variations was notoriously challenging; it was a work more often associated with the harpsichord than the piano; it had been recorded on piano by only two musicians, and one, Rosalyn Tureck, was the established authority. But Gould stood his ground and Columbia gave in.

A few months later, Gould arrived at the recording studio in an abandoned church on East Thirtieth Street in Manhattan. He brought his pygmy chair, a folding bridge chair his father had modified for him in 1953 by sawing four inches off each leg. Gould preferred this chair to any piano bench because it enabled him to sit a perfect fourteen inches off the floor—six inches lower than the height of a standard piano bench. Gould's father fashioned the chair so that it had individually adjustable legs, which enabled Gould to achieve the precise height he wanted on each. The chair had what Gould once referred to as "exactly the right contour." It also had the give Gould wanted in all directions: left, right, forward, backward. It swayed—and creaked—along with him as he moved while playing. The chair was an object that he remained attached to all his life, and he took it with him everywhere. When he traveled for concerts, with or without his own piano, the chair came too, packed in its own travel crate. Another fixture Gould brought with him to the recording sessions was a supply of bottled Poland Spring water, which he believed was the only water fit to drink. He brought pills for headaches, tension, and circulation. And although it was June, of course he arrived in coat, cap, gloves, and muffler. And with those habitual appurtenances he settled into a weeklong recording session of the fabled Goldbergs.

Bach wrote the Goldberg Variations around 1740, some ten years before his death. It is one of the composer's great encyclopedia works—a multifaceted summation of his style. Gould once told an interviewer that while the work was "never high on my hit parade as an integrated experience," it contained some sublime moments for him. Variation 15 in G minor, for instance, one of the canons, was a slow variation that he said moved him "in an extraordinary way" and demonstrated the very best of Bach. And although he had less admiration for the more virtuosic, finger-twisting variations like 5, 14, and 23, those pieces showed off Gould's impeccable technique.

Indeed, Gould's choice of the Goldbergs for his debut record was a shrewd one. Until the time of late Beethoven, the Goldberg Variations was the largest single keyboard work ever written, and through the years the work had acquired a reputation for being unplayable on the piano. But in Gould's agile hands the music became eye-opening, fresh, and brazen. Even those purists who tossed heresy charges at anyone who attempted to play Bach on anything but a harpsichord—who insisted that playing Bach on the piano violated the composer's specific sonoristic intentions—were dumbstruck by what Gould did with Bach on the piano. As David Dubal, a well-known pianist and writer, put it, "Bach on the piano had become a nightmare of boring academic pattern making, full of plushly pedaled un-Baroque sonorities." Gould, in one recording, would change all that.

Gould's approach was part of a general rethinking of how the piano could be used in the service of Bach. By the time Gould came on the scene, a clear, lean style of playing Baroque music, and Bach in particular, was a rising trend, especially among younger pianists. Gould's playing was a particularly dynamic example of this trend and seemed ideally suited to the composer. When Gould played Bach, the music became sparse, abstract, and mysterious. Dubal wrote: "It was a process that went far beyond quibbling about the correct instrument. Indeed, the timbre of the piano under Gould's hands became new and unexpected."

Aside from his sheer technical ability, Gould was giving musical expression to radical beliefs. He argued that the harpsichord purists were suffering from "musicological overkill" and that Bach was comparatively indifferent on the question of which instrument a piece of music was best suited to. When it came to Bach, he argued that in certain circumstances "the piano can get you a lot closer to Bach's conceptual notions than the harpsichord ever can."

Technically, of course, Gould was a breed apart, mostly because of the speed with which his fingers flew. When he was fourteen, his class publication, the 9-D *Bugle*, had dubbed him "the ten hottest fingers in Malvern," Gould's high school. Guerrero had taught him to leave his arms and hands relaxed and let his fingers do as much of the work as possible. And indeed they did. A friend once recalled visiting him at home and watching him sight-read the last movement of Grieg's Piano Concerto at breakneck speed—"like Horowitz, only better," the friend said.

His tactile ability was amazing, yet throughout his career Gould seldom pondered the source of the incredible speed, precision, and dexterity of his hands. He preferred to believe that he was possessed of a mysterious gift that he had no need to understand. When discussing his technique, he offered this Zenlike explanation: At all times, he maintained a mental image of every key on the piano, a tentacular awareness of where each note was and how it would feel to reach for it and strike it. Thereafter, the physical act itself was simple. It was a strategy not unlike the one coaches urge on athletes as they master a sport through a form of visualization. In Gould's case, his skill was aided by an uncanny capacity for memorization. He could read a score through once, then play it flawlessly. And once he had played a piece, years could pass and he could sit down and play it again without hitting a single wrong note.

When performing in public, Gould's choice of programs was always unorthodox. The reigning classical pianists of the day—Vladimir Horowitz, Van Cliburn, Myra Hess, Claudio Arrau—played a more established repertoire founded on the nineteenth-century Romantics. But Gould had no interest in playing such crowd-pleasers. He didn't care about bravura or big, expansive musical gestures.

Gould played pieces by the composers he felt the closest

musical kinship with: Bach, Gibbons, Schoenberg, Berg. And the concertgoing public embraced those choices. Not only was he a critical success, but he was a box-office success as well; his concerts were often sold out months in advance. This wasn't merely amazing on its own. What was more extraordinary was that he managed to play to sold-out houses with such an unusual repertoire. The norm among superstars was something very different. At most, a concert pianist would play Bach as a concert opener. Gould offered Bach as the main course. And he filled concert halls with audiences drawn to the quiet intimacy of his music, which perhaps reminded his listeners of the old teacher's adage: To get people's attention, rather than raise your voice, speak quietly.

Not everyone was thrilled with the newcomer. Rosalyn Tureck was mightily put out by Gould's achievement. As a teenager Tureck had memorized the Goldberg Variations in five weeks, then performed them at Juilliard. The day after her performance, Juilliard's president met Tureck in the corridor and said, still awestruck, "I understood that they weren't possible." "Oh, really?" she replied. Tureck became famous for her pronouncements about the Goldberg Variations. "It is an infinite work of art," she once said. "After the opening aria, the thirty variations traverse the whole experience of man. And the return to the beginning aria at the end is one of the most sublime moments in all art."

She once colorfully described an episode that occurred shortly before she turned seventeen. She lost consciousness, and when she came to, she found herself possessed of a revelation, "an insight into Bach's structure, his musical psychology, his sense of form," and she knew that she had to create an entirely new technique for playing the piano as a result.

It was Tureck who received credit for prying loose from people's minds the conviction that Bach could be played only on a harpsichord. Yet with the advent of Glenn Gould, Tureck's Bach became yesterday's news. Gould's precise articulation combined with the superhuman speed of his fingers made Bach's set of variations take flight. In its attack and phrasing Gould's playing resembled Tureck's, but his tone was more seductive and his approach, especially in terms of rhythm, was more dynamic. His Bach grabbed the public in a way that hers never did. With one recording, Glenn Gould proved that he could play the piano like nobody else in the world. The record caused a sensation among listeners and critics alike, who pronounced him a genius, perhaps the greatest pianist of his generation.

Gould's recording of the Goldberg Variations became the best-selling classical recording of 1956. By 1960, it had sold forty thousand copies, which was, Joseph Roddy noted that year in the *New Yorker*, "just about as astonishing in the record business as a big run on a new edition of the Enneads of Plotinus would be in the book trade." Gould outsold the soundtrack for *The Pajama Game*, one of Columbia's big hits. It even outsold Louis Armstrong. It would eventually become the best-selling classical solo-instrumental album of all time, with sales topping 1.8 million copies. Stardom came to Gould instantaneously. "We know of no pianist like him at any age," wrote Paul Hume in the *Washington Post*. Record-industry publications named Gould's Goldberg Variations the record of the year, then of the decade. Early the following year, at Leonard Bernstein's invitation, Gould played Beethoven's Second Piano Concerto with the New York Philharmonic, and in quick succession recorded Bach Partitas, book two of *The Well-Tempered Clavier*, Beethoven, Brahms, and Haydn. Gould was well on his way to becoming one of the great pianists of the twentieth century.

There was much about Gould's personal appeal that was ineffable. Journalists who interviewed him were invariably impressed by his sharp wit, often at his own expense, his politeness, his charm, and his lack of pretension. And although he wore a tuxedo when performing with orchestras, beginning with the Town Hall recital in 1955, he became the first major pianist to give recitals in a suit, usually unpressed and baggy. His playing exerted an unusual power over his audiences. After seeing Gould perform, or after listening to his records or hearing him on the radio, people swore that they could hear the player's soul and sense its vulnerability. They reported feeling as if their lives had somehow changed. Some who listened to him play Bach said he played it like a prayer; some believed he had a direct link to God.

There was no disregarding Gould's many physical quirks while performing. From the start, audiences were exposed to what Gould preferred to call his "side effects": singing, arm flailing, swaying, and foot stomping. Most conspicuous was his habit of singing aloud as an accompaniment to his own playing. Following a concert in Detroit, the local critic wrote that Gould's humming sounded like "a large blackfly had escaped in the auditorium," recalled Ted Sambell, a technician who for years worked on pianos at the Stratford Festival, where Gould often played in the summer, and had traveled to Detroit to do the tuning for the concert. At times the humming was so pronounced that it seemed a duet was being played between piano and pianist.

Gould sometimes said that he hummed in order to compensate for the shortcomings of an unfamiliar or inferior piano. But he had another explanation for it: It represented wishful thinking, the perfect, ideal phrasing he had in his head that he could never quite achieve in real life. It was probably a little bit of both: The humming expressed his ideal vision of the music he was playing, and it probably became more prominent in situations when an inadequate instrument subverted the realization of that vision.

Fans noticed. A woman once sent a letter to Columbia Records from the Midwest to say she had just bought a recording of Bach's French suites. "Now, you're not going to believe this," she wrote, "but someone is singing in the background as Mr. Gould is playing!" During one of the first recording sessions of the Goldbergs, in fact, Gould's humming was so loud that someone joked that he might consider wearing a gas mask. Playing along, Gould actually picked up a gas mask at a war-surplus store and, as a gag, wore it at the start of his next session.

Beyond the vocal accompaniment, Gould stomped, swayed in time to the music, and conducted himself whenever he had a free hand. He sat sidesaddle much of the time, with one knee almost on the floor. He insisted on using the wobbly little fold-up chair so he wouldn't be too far above the keys. As if the effect of the chair weren't enough, he also spent considerable time having small, custom-built wooden blocks, about 1.25 inches high, placed under each piano leg to uniformly raise the height of the entire instrument.

Gould was by no means the only high-level pianist with a tic or two. Rudolf Serkin rocked and squirmed when he played, and whacked the pedal with his foot. The Russian pianist Vladimir de Pachmann mugged and chattered and pantomimed his way through concerts. Self-accompaniment was not so unusual, either. Toscanini once sang his way through a recorded broadcast of La Bohème, Pablo Casals hummed and grunted through the Bach suites for unaccompanied cello, and the jazz pianist Keith Jarrett became famous for his audible moans during concerts. All things considered, Gould was not so very different from the others—just louder.

There was a touch of Beatlemania to some of the adoration of the handsome young pianist. Scores of young women wrote fan letters with pointed questions. Was he single? Interested? Might he agree to a meeting? One woman went so far as to show up at Columbia Records in New York, hoping for a chance meeting. Another wrote to him regularly for years, pouring her heart out in each letter.

The features that distinguished Gould's idiosyncratic piano playing made him extremely particular about his pianos. He demanded something very different from what a generic, standard-issue piano provided. Instead of volume he required nuance; rather than sustaining power, he needed incisiveness.

He was seldom happy with one piano for very long. When Gould was a child, his father bought new instruments—first uprights, then a series of grands—at regular intervals. And as Gould grew older, he took over the search for playable instruments. One happy discovery he made was a piano that became an ideal against which he measured the various concert pianos he would encounter for the rest of his life. It was a small grand made in 1895 by the Boston-based firm Chickering. Gould had discovered the Chickering in 1954, when it was in the possession of a friend who was renting it. It was a well-decorated instrument, with stout, carved legs, an ornamented lyre above the pedals, and a richly carved music desk. Based on looks alone, the Chickering would have fit very nicely in a well-appointed parlor. But Gould had no interest in the piano's appearance. He loved its touch.

Gould liked the piano so much, in fact, that he took over the rental and finally bought it outright in 1957. He did most of his practicing for the U.S. debut on the Chickering, its tactile immediacy a perfect fit with his musical tastes. But although the Chickering was his ideal instrument, he knew it was a piano he could never perform concerts on. Not only was it too small to project the kind of sound needed in a concert hall (by and large, concert pianists never perform on anything but a nine-foot concert grand), but the piano produced a distinct banjolike twang.

Still, the Chickering clarified for him the features he wanted as he continued to seek a concert grand. For a time it seemed he had found the perfect instrument: CD 174, a piano with a featherlight action that felt just right under his fingers. He had chanced upon it at Steinway one day in 1955, when both the piano and the pianist happened to be in the same place at the same time. Gould loved CD 174 so much he used it to record the Goldberg Variations. But he didn't have the piano for very long, and it would be several years before he would find another concert grand that felt just right under his hyperdiscerning touch.

TWO

Saskatchewan

*Verne Edquist at age eight on his auntie
Fromme's farm in rural Saskatchewan, with
his aunt's cat Trölse.* Courtesy of Verne
Edquist.

The person who would eventually infuse an instrument with all that Glenn Gould desired was a poor, nearly blind farm boy.

Charles Verne Edquist was born in 1931, a year before Gould, in a little farming district in Saskatchewan called Glen Mary, four hundred miles north of the Montana border. The province was reeling from crop failures, and poverty was the central fact of Verne's early childhood. His father, Charley, a burly Swedish immigrant who had worked his way over to Canada with a job as a deckhand on a cattle boat, had a penchant for troublemaking—frequently involving too much drinking and brawling. When Verne was a toddler, Charley was deported back to Sweden. His mother, Thea, who like Verne's father had come to Canada in 1905 as part of a stream of Swedish immigrants, was left to raise her children on her own. As soon as her family began to grow, Thea took work as a live-in housekeeper in order to have a place to put her family. When Verne was two, the family moved into an abandoned farmhouse—his older sister called it the Snake Pit because the property was filled with garter snakes—where his baby sister died at the age of eleven months.

Then came a series of moves. Life became a blur of different farmhouses where meals consisted mostly of porridge made from oatmeal, potatoes, and milk, and good drinking water was hard to come by. Fruit—rhubarb and saskatoon berries if the rain came—was a rare treat. Finally, unable to provide for her three children, Thea sent Verne's ten-year-old brother to live with another family, where he performed farm chores in exchange for room and board.

It was Verne's uncle Hjalmar who first noticed that Verne, then six years old, was having trouble seeing. One freezing winter morning a cousin took Verne by train to a doctor sixty miles away in Prince Albert. He was diagnosed with congenital cataracts. A few weeks later he was taken back, this time for surgery. The train, which had a snowplow attached to the front of the engine, was like a loud, frightening monster, but Verne didn't find it nearly as terrifying as the experience that followed in the doctor's office. He was given chloroform and strapped to the operating table, and the surgeon needled the lens inside the eye to break the cataracts up into smaller particles so that natural enzymes might absorb them. Though a common form of surgery at the time, needling seldom restored full vision. Although Verne's eyesight was somewhat improved, it remained minimal for the rest of his life.

Sounds and smells were the prism through which young Verne came to experience the world: the wind whistling through the telephone wires, the loud, clanging merry-go-round at the local fair. To this day Edquist can recall the sound of a neighbor's labored breathing, an old man who had been gassed in the First World War. On very cold nights, when the temperature dropped to forty degrees below zero, he could hear the black poplars cracking from the frost and could smell a man in buckskin clothing who passed by, driving a dog team, to peddle frozen fish. And there was the constant odor of weasel skins being cured by his older cousins, which they later sold to a local fur dealer.

Each season had a distinctive aroma and its own set of sounds. In the winter the sounds were the sleigh runners squeaking in the snow, wagon wheels on the road, and coyotes howling in the distance. The smell was of heavy wool socks drying near the stove. In spring it was the black soil warming and the sound of returning crows. Summer brought the smell of the poplars and the sounds of rustling leaves, frogs croaking in sloughs, and cattle being set out to pasture. In the summer came the grasshoppers, which made an articulated clicking noise when they flew. When someone was milking a cow, he could tell how full the pail was from the way it sounded. But there was one sound that would haunt Verne for years: the screams of a boy whose younger brother had drowned in a shallow well. For the rest of his life, he would remember the boy's panicked cries as he ran looking for his aunt to tell her what had happened.

A few months after the surgery a pair of glasses arrived in the mail, and for the first time the boy was able to see shapes at a distance—leaves on trees and the outlines of objects. Colors became more prominent, and over the years Verne used color association not merely to help him remember things but to explain the world. Later, when learning arithmetic, he saw numbers as colors: Two was green, three was silver, four was orange, five was pink, and six was blue. Fifty-six was a pinkish blue. He even began viewing intangible concepts in colors. The month of December was a bright yellow. June was blue. Verne had a form of synesthesia, a neurological condition in which two or more senses are coupled. But rather than detract from his ability to navigate the world around him, the synesthesia helped him to organize and understand his surroundings. Still, with less than 10 percent of his vision intact, he could not see well enough to attend the local school.

When Verne was seven, his aunt and uncle gave his mother three acres of land, and Uncle Hjalmar built them a two-room house. Hjalmar spent weeks hammering nails in a steady, methodical, rhythmic way. It was the young boy's introduction to percussive rhythm, and for years afterward when he heard that particular two-beat rhythm in music he would associate it with expert carpentry. In later years, whenever he passed a construction site, he would be appalled to hear the sound of random hammering, which signaled to his sensitive ears that ham-fisted craftsmen were at work.

In the winter of 1938, deep into the Depression, Verne's mother found it harder and harder to fend for her family. Food was increasingly scarce. The cow grew ill and had to be slaughtered. After months of drought the prairie farmers gazed at endless stretches of barren fields. Thea received five dollars a month in Relief Allowance, but the fact that she had not put her boy in school was rankling the town's councilors, who warned her that the money would be cut off if she did not do something about her son's education. To be sure, with its bitter winters and scorched, barren summers, Depression-era Saskatchewan was no place for a nearly blind boy who was not attending school. One day that summer, a large shiny coupe drove up to the house. Its driver, an official with the child welfare office, consulted with Thea and told her he had made arrangements for Verne to be sent away to a school for the blind. The province of Saskatchewan, he told her, would pay all of the boy's expenses. In early September, his older sister, who worked as a maid, borrowed money against her wages to buy school clothes for him. His cousins taught him the proper words to use for the washroom. His older brother, Johnnie, who was on a harvest crew, came by the night before his departure. Verne had always relied on his brother, who was eight years older, to teach him some basics about life— hygiene, manners, and other social niceties. That night, Johnnie sent Verne off with some of the best advice he had: If you have any candy, share it. The next morning, eight-year-old Verne, anxious but suitably attired, was put on a train and sent two thousand miles east to the Ontario School for the Blind in Brantford. His mother wept as she gave him his ticket, seventeen cents, and a small suitcase, and promised that the conductor would look after him.

The train took him as far as Regina, the capital of Saskatchewan, where he spent the night at an orphanage. The next morning he was put on another train, and at noon he was

ushered into the dining car for a meal that was like none he had
ever eaten: ham with raisin sauce, potatoes, and cauliflower. A
new sound, the light, clear ringing of ice water in a glass, would
carry pleasant associations for the rest of his life.

In Winnipeg a car took him to another train station where he
boarded yet another train. Gradually, others who were headed
to the school for blind children started boarding, and by the
time the train got to central Ontario there were enough students to fill two cars.

Set in a remote part of Brantford, a small city of knitting
mills and foundries in southern Ontario, the school was a self-
sufficient operation where the students were pressed into service harvesting crops and milking cows. As soon as Verne
arrived, the grubby youngster was marched straight to the first
shower of his life, handed a bar of carbolic soap, and told to
scrub himself until he was clean.

The Ontario School for the Blind was Verne's introduction to
life among other children like himself. Upon meeting each
other, new students would share their age and grade and explain
how they came to be blind. One boy, born in a log cabin in
Saskatchewan a few years before Verne, explained that the doctor who had delivered him had neglected to carry silver nitrate
drops to prevent eye infections. A girl had been kicked by a
horse, her optic nerve severed. Another had been stabbed in the
eye with a pitchfork. Another had a brain tumor. Like Verne,
several classmates had congenital cataracts.

Despite the fact that he was finally among other children
who shared his disability, within a month or two the boy grew
homesick and lonely. The school's philosophy mixed austerity
with exhortation, and the teachers were known for pep talks
filled with aphorisms aimed at discouraging self-pity: "If you
want to accomplish something, get out there and do it." "Trou-
bles can be a challenge." "The man who never made a mistake

never did anything." And the school's motto: "The impossible is only the untried." These maxims were intended to inject self-confidence in a group of children whose colossal disadvantage in life had stripped them of a few basic assumptions that sighted children possessed. The "untried" could mean the simple daring act of climbing a tree, or running a foot race. Verne was moved by the mottoes from the moment he heard them, and he would recite them like bedtime prayers for years afterward.

Institutionalized blind students from among the poor were usually taught handcrafts, and the school in Brantford focused on a variety of trades. The students made rubber mats out of old tires and wove baskets from willow reeds grown, harvested, and dried at the school's farm. They recaned chairs sent from all over Canada, assembled locks, repaired shoes, and made brooms. Girls at the school learned typing, sewing, and home economics.

Soon after he arrived, Verne heard a sound he had encountered only once before, back home in Saskatchewan. It was probably at one of the houses his mother worked in, where there was a radio. It was a piano, and when he asked his sister what created the sound it made, she told him she thought it was bells. Now all over the school came a constant stream of sound from a half dozen different pianos, which students played with varying degrees of proficiency. In time he grew accustomed to the sound. And he liked it. He liked hearing the different pitches, and he quickly discovered his ear could easily distinguish one from the other. It wasn't until he contracted scarlet fever and spent six weeks in the hospital, some of it by himself in quarantine, feeling very lonely, that he heard a different piano sound. It was a pinging, not quite musical and hardly melodic. Mystified, and thinking his fever might be playing tricks with his hearing, Verne asked a nurse what it was. She explained that the school hospital was near the shop where students learned how to tune pianos. What he was hearing were the strange sounds produced when the intervals between notes are stretched and compressed. The sound was by turns pleasant and abrasive. He was intrigued. He lay in bed, drifting in and out of sleep, the tone of the pianos never far away. Sometimes the sounds entered his dreams.

THE FIRST BLIND piano tuner is thought to have been Claude Montal, a man who taught himself how to tune a piano in the 1820s while attending a school for the blind in Paris. With a fellow student, young Montal had found a derelict piano, disassembled it, repaired it, put it together again, and tuned it. Convincing his teachers of his proficiency, Montal demonstrated that blindness and piano tuning could go hand in hand. He started teaching his fellow students and eventually became a tuner for professional musicians. Montal's success paved the way for other blind tuners. In 1869, Thomas Rhodes Armitage, an influential British doctor who was an early supporter of braille and braille music, paid a visit to Montal's Parisian school, where tuning had become a mainstay of the curriculum. Dr. Armitage returned to England and helped spread his enthusiasm for the value of teaching piano tuning to the blind instead of, say, weaving mats and baskets. By the beginning of the twentieth century, schools for the blind around the world were integrating piano tuning into their curricula. Piano tuning, perhaps more than any other profession for the blind, soon offered a way past a handicap and into the working world.

Piano tuning as a trade was first institutionalized in piano factories in Europe before it emerged as a freestanding profession in the late nineteenth century. By that time the piano had become an indispensable status symbol in upper-middle-class households, but the instruments were far too complex for the average owner to keep in tune. Professional tuners came to occupy a special position: They were tradesmen who hailed from the factory floor, yet they were welcomed into people's homes to work on what was often regarded as a family's prized possession.

In the United States after World War II, piano tuning became a competitive profession for sighted and blind men alike, as trade schools popped up all over the place to train veterans under the G.I. Bill of Rights, also known as the Serviceman's Readjustment Act of 1944. Some of the G.I.s at these schools had been blinded in combat and sought to learn a trade that didn't require the use of their eyes. Often they were taught alongside their sighted classmates.

Emil Fries, a blind technician who in 1949 started a tuning school for the blind in Washington State, became a tireless advocate for blind tuners and even refused to teach at schools that mixed blind students with sighted ones. He once wrote, "The principle of having to teach both the blind and the seeing students would, I am sure, be the final and complete sell-out of the blind. The seeing now have at least fifteen recognized schools of piano tuning to choose from, plus stores and factories where they can be taught. Practically none of these are open to the blind. Experience has taught me that it is not easy to place a blind graduate and the position would many times go to the sighted man, even though he had much less training and real knowledge of the piano." In the blind community, Fries, known to some as "the man who saved piano tuning for the blind," became famous for this stance. In his zeal, he perhaps overstated the case, as blind piano tuners continued to train and be placed in jobs alongside the sighted.

At the Ontario School for the Blind, tuning was taught as an extra subject after school and was widely considered a pursuit for boys. Many of the girls lacked the strength to lift the action out of a piano or to apply enough torque to turn the pins. To the school administrators, signing up for piano-tuning classes was a sign of ambition. But it wasn't ambition that motivated Verne Edquist; it was the fear of what would happen to him if he were to return to Saskatchewan without a useful trade. He was determined to avoid a life spent sitting idly on someone's doorstep, which he imagined was the fate that awaited him if he went home untrained.

So in 1944, the year twelve-year-old Glenn Gould won his first piano trophy by playing Bach at the Kiwanis Music Festival in Toronto, Edquist entered seventh grade at the Ontario School for the Blind and began learning how to tune pianos.

The starting point for a new student is the tuning of unisons, the three strings that, when played together, form one note. The tuner's aim is to have all three strings sound as one note when the hammer strikes. After he learned to tune a unison, Verne moved on to octaves, all the while refining his sense of hearing. The beginning students practiced on giant old uprights, the kind of cheap no-name instruments that people bought for a dollar down and a dollar a week. Some were more difficult to tune than others. Age is often a factor, as is the quality of the piano. After a year or two of working on these clunkers, students were sent off to tune the music teachers' pianos, which seemed easy compared to the monstrous, worn-out uprights in the shop. The teacher also brought in zithers from a local factory, fifty at a time, and the students tuned them for fifty cents apiece and were allowed to keep the money.

But Verne didn't progress quickly in the tuning shop. Indeed, piano tuning is a colossally difficult job. It is a skill often handed down through generations, and a rule of thumb says it takes years—and at least a thousand pianos—to learn to do it correctly. And once you've achieved a certain level of proficiency, it can take several more years to rise to the more exalted level of concert tuner. Years later, Edquist would say that he tuned for ten years before he felt he was getting somewhere.

A skilled tuner possesses not just a good ear but also the ability to distinguish the smallest differences in tone and pitch across a piano's entire keyboard, from the lowest snarling bass to the high, shimmering treble notes. Although there are just eighty-eight keys, a piano has some 230 strings, since most notes have three strings—and each string must be set to a particular pitch, which must in turn relate to the pitch of all the other strings.

Standard pitch is fixed at A440 hertz, or cycles per second, meaning that the A above middle C is adjusted so that the string oscillates 440 times each second. That is how the note gets its distinctive pitch. But if the rest of the piano were tuned in direct mathematical proportion to that note, it would sound dissonant. In order to play most of the music composed in the last few hundred years, a keyboard instrument must be tuned using what is known as an "equal temperament" system. That is, the twelve semitones of the chromatic scale are more or less equal in size so that music in any key sounds equally in tune. On a piano tuned in equal temperament, a pianist can modulate from C major to F-sharp major to A-flat minor without any of the intervals sounding off. At the same time, even equal temperament is still a compromise because it is not mathematically or acoustically possible to have equal temperament with pure intervals. (On a piano, the only intervals that are in fact pure are octaves.) As a result, a tuner ends up making a series of compromises: A fifth gets compressed a little bit, a fourth gets expanded, and so forth. The result is that the degree of pureness is generally acceptable to the ear, and the piano can play equally harmoniously in any key. The tuner's art is to find a balance between the mathematically pure and the musically pleasing so the average person cannot tell the difference.

Equal temperament may seem to go without saying, but early music—say, before 1700—tended to be written in a far more limited range of keys than modern music. One rarely saw more than three sharps or flats in a piece of music. This meant that a tuner could take into account the fact that the musician would not need equal access to all keys. For instance, if a musician was playing something in C major on the harpsichord, the instrument could be tuned so that the intervals in C major (and closely related keys like A minor and G major) were closer to pure than they could be in equal temperament. Anything in F-sharp major played on that instrument would sound sour. Then again, back in the 1600s, a piece written in C major never modulated to F-sharp major or any other distant key.

Each instrument has to be tuned differently, because the length, diameter, and tension of the piano wire varies with every piano, which is what gives each instrument its unique tonal profile. And every tuner has a personal preference in terms of the acoustic compromises he is willing to make to get an equally tempered scale that sounds good in both melodic and harmonic playing. So it isn't at all unusual for someone with a good ear to be able to pick out a particular tuner's system.

A steady hand is another essential, and this is where blind piano tuners, who often have a highly developed sense of touch, enjoy an advantage over their sighted colleagues. Skilled tuners can feel a good tuning as much as they can hear it. Turning the tuning wrench as little as possible to reach the desired pitch is a much harder task than it might seem, for the hand and arm must learn to feel the minute gradations of pitch that are achieved by the slightest turns of the tuning pin. There are musicians who believe that the best tuners are the ones who turn the pins the least.

It is hard and demanding work. In addition to all these skills—physical strength, a steady hand, an acutely sensitive ear—the piano tuner must also have the abiding patience to accept, and even anticipate, that once a piano is tuned, it immediately starts to go out of tune again. Some pianos stay in tune better than others. "To a novice, it's almost impossible," said Edquist. "You need patience to stick it out and not quit. It takes years of practice to make a string hold its pitch when played firmly."

In the early 1900s, when men were flocking to the profession, some found the constant exposure to loud, often dissonant tones unbearable. In 1904, a tuner in England appeared in court after being sued for outstanding debts, and when the judge asked him why he was out of work, the man replied that he had had to give up tuning, as it had nearly caused him to lose his sanity. "It was such a dreadful noise," he complained. In the early twentieth century, piano tuners outnumbered members of any other trade in English insane asylums.

Although he was advancing in his tuning studies by the time he was twelve, Verne was less than dedicated to other classwork, preferring the outdoors, where he and his schoolmates made up their own games, to the classroom. One game started with a boy in the middle of the sidewalk who tried to touch people as they ran by. As boys got tagged, they too became taggers, until eventually one person was left trying to circle the entire group without being touched. From these games the blind and nearly blind boys cultivated a highly developed sense of space and were able to gauge the distance—the inches and the feet of empty space—between two objects. They could even sense when a void had been filled with a solid object, or was about to be filled. Said Edquist, "We had blind guys and you'd think they could see."

While many of his schoolmates also learned to play the piano, Verne never did. It wasn't for lack of trying. His teacher, Miss Perry, required that her students learn to read music in braille, which meant that in order to play the piano they would first hold the page and run their fingers along it, reading the music, then put the page down and play the notes they had read on the keyboard. Naturally this put a premium on memorization. She also taught her students to write music in braille, and as part of the discipline they were required to write a piece and then play it from memory on the spot. "I just wasn't that good at memorizing," Edquist recalled later. "And I wasn't a good braille reader to begin with." Some of his fellow students, on the other hand, excelled at both braille and memorization. One boy memorized a concerto in bed and played it the next day, but Verne recalled that he played without feeling, which went to the heart of the problem of his teacher's pedagogical approach: She focused on technical ability rather than soul. Even when Verne played in an assembly for his fellow students, Miss Perry was unable to keep her disappointment to herself, and humiliated him with her criticism. Verne kept up his studies, but even decades later it was with some psychological pain that he recalled the hours spent in Miss Perry's classroom. A good teacher can inspire, but a bad teacher can crush a fragile young ego like Verne's, and he never quite recovered from the experience. Playing the piano was, clearly, not to be part of his future. Eventually he switched instruments and chose to play the trombone and the upright bass to satisfy the school's music requirements. But *listening* to the piano, and learning to distinguish the nuances of tone that were unrecognizable to most human ears, would become his livelihood.

VERNE RETURNED HOME to Saskatchewan every summer to see his family and work on the farm, but everywhere he went he would find reminders of the implacable destitution there. He always looked forward to returning to school, but the year that he returned to Ontario to begin the eleventh grade he was told that his marks were not high enough to advance with the rest of his class. Verne panicked, terrified that he would be thrown out of school with no prospects for employment. He knew of several students who had left the Ontario School for the Blind to work at Ford, doing wheel assembly, but he was warned by his shop teacher that a job in a production line would be difficult and monotonous, and he dismissed the idea. He thought about traveling to the U.S. to take a course in electric motors but didn't have enough money to get there, much less enroll.

Out of desperation, Verne turned back to piano tuning, this time in earnest, hoping to gain a place in grade eleven. He did. And he began studying with a rigor and determination that few teachers there had seen. When Verne set to tuning a piano, his concentration grew fierce, and he was both inspired and motivated by his teacher, J. D. Ansell. Years later Verne would still quote Ansell's favorite axiom: "The only place where success comes before work is in the dictionary." To broaden his young protégé's experience, Ansell took him into town to tune pianos in people's homes. He was allowed to keep the money—$2.50 per piano and sometimes, when he got lucky, $3—which he put toward some basic tools: a tuning wrench, a tuning fork, needle-nose pliers, gauges for measuring the diameter of piano wire, and rubber wedges for muting strings.

Verne immersed himself so thoroughly in tuning that he began to dream about it. One night he dreamed that he had landed a job as head tuner at Heintzman, the most prominent piano manufacturer in Canada. The dream stayed with him for months afterward.

Even among other blind students, he had certain natural advantages. For one thing, he could hear eerily fine distinctions in sound. He could tell the make and model of a car by the sound of its engine. Well into his career, if he was listening to a piano recording, he could recognize if the tuning was his own. Also, while learning to tune, Edquist discovered he had excellent, nearly perfect pitch. And all his life, just as he saw numbers and seasons in colors, he heard music with the same odd synesthetic mixing of the senses. If you asked him how he knew that an F was an F, he would say, "Oh, that's blue." C was a slightly lime green. The key of D was a sandy hue, E was a yellowy pink, A was white, G orange, and B dark green. For years he was ashamed of this unorthodox practice, and he didn't tell anyone about it until he was older, when he confided in Glenn Gould—who reacted as if it were the most natural phenomenon in the world.

He knew that his best chance at a job straight out of school was to find work as a chipper in one of Toronto's dozen or so piano factories. Chippers are the first tuners to work on a newly strung piano, and they begin their work when the instrument is only partly complete, even before it has a keyboard. At this stage the strings are not necessarily aligned with the hammers, so the initial tunings are done by plucking the strings with a small chip of wood—hence the term *chippers*.

So in 1950, at age nineteen and with diploma in hand and forty dollars in his pocket—a loan from the school's principal— Edquist boarded a train to Toronto with a sense that he could take on the world. In one hand he carried a suitcase and in the other a fishing-tackle box he had converted to a tuner's toolbox. Over the years he would collect dozens of tools. Some he bought from old-timers, and others he adapted from other trades. He had surgical forceps and dental explorers, which made excellent hooks; optician's screwdrivers for adjusting harpsichords; barber's scissors for trimming felt; and shoemaker's pegs for plugging holes. From the welding trade he took soapstone, a dry lubricant to stop the buckskin in the action of older pianos from squeaking.

As soon as Edquist arrived in Toronto, he took the tuning test required by the Canadian National Institute for the Blind. The man administering the test was Sanford Leppard, the first tuner to graduate from the Ontario School for the Blind, in 1882. Leppard was now elderly but still a grand and imposing figure. "I thought he was Methuselah when he came in there, and I was scared skinny," Edquist later recalled. He passed the exam and began his career as an apprentice chipper in the Toronto factory of the Winter Company, a subsidiary of a large, reputable piano maker, Mason & Risch, which was rumored to have been purchased in the 1940s by two taxi drivers from New York. But while a Mason & Risch instrument was a solid piano, the mainstay of a well-off Canadian, Winter's pianos were of lesser quality and far more difficult to tune.

The factory turned out to be something of a sweatshop. The work was hard and dirty. Near the end of the first day, as Edquist was working on his fourth piano, the foreman came around and told him that any number fewer than nine pianos was unacceptable. "I thought, Do I stay here, or do I quit?" Edquist later recalled.

Edquist was discouraged, but he didn't quit. Paid by the piece, he soon learned how to work quickly—and before long he was tuning ten pianos a day. He disliked working this way, because he often found himself spending extra time correcting mistakes that had been made up the line by another worker. Still, within two weeks he had earned enough to pay back the forty-dollar loan from the school principal who had subsidized his trip to Toronto.

The visually impaired tuners at Winter's were known as either "gawkers" or "gropers." Technically, Verne Edquist was a gawker: someone with less than 10 percent vision. Gropers were totally blind. And gawkers could often be found staring intensely at something in order to make it out. For all the time he

had spent at a school for the blind, and for all the daily con-
frontations with the limitations of his visual impairment, he
was still reluctant to come to terms with the fact that he was
nearly blind. So when he arrived at Winter's he tried gawking
for the first month or so, straining to see the tuning pins in order
to place the lever on them, his head nearly inside the piano. His
boss, a sympathetic man who had supervised dozens of blind
tuners, recognized the effort that Edquist was making and
showed him how to tune without looking. In fact, the supervi-
sor promised, feeling his way through the piano would enable
the young tuner to do a better job, as he wouldn't be distracted
by the limits of his eyesight. Edquist took the man's advice and
found that it made a huge difference. He soon became adept at
shutting out the distractions of the shop, which were considerable since the pianos were tuned in the same room where they
were built. The room was dusty from the sanding machines and
noisy from the pneumatic drills, but Edquist found that if he
concentrated hard enough, he could feel and hear his way
through the din to a decent tuning. "If you learn how to tune in
the factory," he said later, "you can tune anywhere."

This same fellow who converted Verne from a gawker told
him after a few weeks that he was doing a better job than the
floor boss, a sighted man who had been there for years. Indeed,
tuning was developing into something of an obsession: Edquist
found he was in competition with himself, racing to give as
many pianos as possible a respectable tuning. Once he settled
into a rhythm he made thirty-five dollars a week, and gradually
his ambition grew. He made up his mind to someday work at a
more distinguished factory, where he could learn the fine points
of the trade from the old-timers.

After a few months in Toronto, he went home to visit his
mother in Saskatchewan. He was struck more forcibly than ever
by how impoverished the place was, and how fortunate he was

to have found a way out. Ironically, he realized, it was his visual impairment that had paved the way for his escape. And although he knew there were countless aesthetic satisfactions that would forever remain beyond his reach—painting, photography, and all the other visual arts that can't be experienced through anything but the eyes—all it took was one trip back to Saskatchewan to remind him of his good fortune. Edquist now considered Toronto his home, and the trip back to Saskatchewan made him more appreciative than ever of the opportunities the urban center held. But when he returned to Toronto he faced more bad news: He had been laid off from his tuning job. Saskatchewan was cursed, he decided. Even going home for a visit brought bad luck.

HAVING LOST HIS job, Edquist decided to simply knock on doors to find work tuning. He knew that most families had a piano and that few of them went to the trouble of having it tuned. He was systematic in his approach, choosing a sequence of different neighborhoods around Toronto that he could reach by streetcar. When people opened their doors and saw the earnest young man standing on the doorstep holding his tool bag, peering at them from behind glasses with impossibly thick lenses, they often responded skeptically. How could they know he would do a good job? "Well, I've had some training and I'll do the best I can," he promised, and explained that good eyesight has precious little to do with tuning a piano. Once he got down to work, doubts would fade.

Now more than ever he was glad he had made the switch from gawker to groper because, as he soon discovered, "when you go over to somebody's house, you look more confident when you're not staring at the pins." The pianos Edquist encountered were in various states of tonal disrepair. Some had been forgotten in the corner of a back parlor, the fallboard down, objects strewn on the bench. Others were clearly well tended to and well played. Those were the instruments he enjoyed tuning the most, as he could sense how they had been broken in, even what kind of music was played on them, just from how the tuning progressed.

Growing bolder, Edquist began cold-calling at sergeants' messes, insane asylums, and prisons. He would walk a mile and a half in a snowstorm to tune a piano for three dollars. He was lucky to get one tuning a day.

Then, as so often happened with him, from the hard luck emerged good. When he grew tired of tramping the streets, he started hanging around piano shops doing odd jobs, which led to a series of informal apprenticeships with various piano tuners in Toronto. The most important was with Henry Kneifel, a middle-aged man who had been trained in Vienna as a Steinway concert tuner. Edquist was happy to do odd jobs for Kneifel— sweep the floors, do the occasional tuning on pianos Kneifel couldn't be bothered with—as long as he could watch and listen as Kneifel worked. Kneifel also taught the younger man how to fine-tune a piano and showed him the rudiments of tone regulating, a skill Edquist had yet to learn and would wait years before attempting himself.

Tone regulating, or voicing a piano, is entirely different from action regulating, and altogether distinct from tuning. A tone regulator focuses on the density of the hammer felt and its relationship to the string. A good tone regulator, Edquist learned from Kneifel, has extremely acute hearing. Whereas a tuner listens for variations in pitch, a tone regulator listens for subtle variations in tone quality. And while a tuner employs a tuning fork as a guide, the tone regulator uses his memory of a sound to guide him. Kneifel taught Edquist the concept of good tone, and the young tuner was soon able to strike a note on the piano and remember the lingering harmonic tones the way a wine expert can summon from memory the aromas that are released in the lingering finish of a good wine. It was learning this skill that would catapult him beyond the realm of mere tuner and into the realm of technician, a more rarefied calling.

It was in Kneifel's shop that Edquist grew familiar with Steinways and came to appreciate the craftsmanship that went into building them. Kneifel had an odd but also awe-inspiring ritual he engaged in after rebuilding a Steinway. He took a leather-encased iron weight, held it in his fist, and pounded each of the eighty-eight keys four or five times. He explained that this was the way they did it at Steinway, so that any key that was going to break would break and could be fixed then and there—a circumstance far preferable to having a key break in the middle of a Rachmaninoff piano concerto.

It was from Kneifel that Edquist started to develop opinions about other makes of piano. Steinways, he learned, were beautifully engineered instruments. Heintzman built the best upright, a piano people would pay a year's wages to own. And Mason & Hamlin grand pianos were among the finest, with extra weight in their rims and plates. They were preferred by some tuners over the Steinways: In fact, the Mason & Hamlin factory in Rochester, New York, was considered a utopia for tuners. "You were given enough time to do the job correctly," Edquist recalled.

In 1952, the dream young Verne had while at the Ontario School for the Blind came true. At the age of twenty-one he was hired as the chief fine-tuner in the Heintzman factory, responsible for the tuning and regulating of all the newly finished grand pianos. Heintzman was Canada's Steinway & Sons, the country's premiere piano manufacturer. The factory had eight floors of pianos with 250 instruments on each floor, plus a full-blown concert department that kept a dozen tuners on the road at all times, accompanying touring pianists around the world.

Bill Heintzman was good to his workers. He bought Edquist a five-hundred-dollar savings bond and let him collect the interest. When another tuner arrived from England, Heintzman took out a mortgage for him so he could buy a house. Still, he worked his men hard and the days at Heintzman were long: Workers had to punch the clock before seven A.M., and if they were three minutes late they were docked fifteen.

At Heintzman, the young tuner was put in charge of people twice his age, mostly blind men who had been working on pianos for decades, and he found that he had a lot to learn from them. "They didn't have a lot of education, but they had a lot of wisdom," he said. "It just happened that I had a good tuning teacher, and I knew about fine-tuning, and those guys who did rough factory tuning didn't." Having switched from factory tuning to concert tuning, Edquist was working on fewer pianos now. Instead of ten pianos each day, he was tuning only four or five. But each had to be perfect.

Edquist had been at Heintzman for three years when, late one afternoon in 1955, a buzz permeated the building as the most famous Canadian pianist of the day entered, chair in hand. Twenty-three-year-old Glenn Gould had stopped by to try out some of the pianos for a CBC program he was doing, and he proceeded directly to Heintzman's sixth floor, where there was an artists' room with four or five concert grands set up for musicians to play. In 1955 Gould was still all but unknown outside of Canada, but that would have been surprising news to the Heintzman employees, many of whom stopped what they were doing and strained to hear as Gould, dressed in his bulky winter overcoat, cap, and fingerless gloves, played every piano on the floor. The tuner kept his distance as others crowded around outside the elevators.

Gould grazed his way through the pianos. As a salesman hovered nearby with his chair, the musician approached each instrument and played a few measures while still standing. If he was displeased, he simply moved on. If he wanted a little more time with a piano, the salesman placed the chair before the instrument and Gould kept playing. Edquist vividly remembered the low figure Gould cut as he sat before each piano, peering over the keyboard like a small boy gazing across a fence. From the fawning attentiveness Gould received, Edquist sensed for the first time the effects of fame, which made the piano tuner uncomfortable. The afternoon also gave the tuner his first taste of many of Glenn Gould's odd traits, which would become so familiar over the years: the desire to be left alone competing with a desire to be the center of attention, and the strange clothes he wore, which immediately gave him away. "There was no mistaking him," Edquist remembered later. The two men did not interact that day, yet as Edquist stood nearby, listening, he thought to himself that he was still many years away from being able to tune for an artist like Glenn Gould.

Thus was Edquist motivated to make regular visits to Kneifel's shop so he could continue to refine his craft and learn from the older man. By now he had focused his ambition on the pinnacle of his trade: tuning for concert pianists. Something about the brief appearance of Glenn Gould in his life emboldened him to think it might not be too presumptuous to aspire to concert tuning, perhaps even tuning Steinways for someone as accomplished as Gould. Kneifel encouraged Edquist, but warned the young tuner that it would be a long time before he would be able to tune a concert grand—any concert grand—in under two hours, the accepted standard among concert tuners.

And indeed it took five years of intense work. But by 1961 Edquist had been hired as the chief concert tuner at Eaton's, the Steinway dealer for all of Canada. Even with a dozen years of tuning at Heintzman, Edquist was required to take a tuning test for the Eaton's job. But the salary, seventy-five dollars a week, was a good fifteen dollars more than he had been making as the fine-tuner in the Heintzman factory. The test was, of course, a formality. His tuning had always stood out, even when he was a novice. And to trained ears, the quality of Edquist's tuning was always superior. He could have moved to New York and held his own against the best tuners there, but Canada was his home. He knew his way around Toronto, he knew the names of the streets, he knew the streetcar system and the bus routes, and he knew which parts of town to avoid.

And he had met the woman he planned to marry: Lillian Lilholt, a young Sunday school teacher at a Lutheran church in Toronto.

At Eaton's, Edquist was put on a salary for the first time in his working life. Now every week he received an envelope containing cash, always the correct amount. Still better, he could go to other departments inside Eaton's and buy the basic furnishings, appliances, and bedding he needed for his new family without having to pay interest.

In Eaton's stable, the handful of Steinways differed from one another in small, idiosyncratic, often unpredictable ways. Some were difficult to keep in tune, their intervals shifting a few hours after a tuning. CD 226 was by far the worst. In Edquist's opinion, it was a dog of a piano. Occasionally, long after he had gone home for the day and settled into his evening routine, he would get a call from Muriel Mussen, the concert manager at Eaton's, asking him to call a taxi and come over right away because so and so, who was in town for a concert, found CD 226 unplayable. Eventually CD 226 was returned to New York, but only after Clifford Gray, the head of Eaton's piano department, personally intervened with Steinway.

Other pianos were unusually compliant, holding a tuning for three or four concerts and still coming back in tune, in need of just a little smoothing out before returning to the stage.

There was something about Edquist's tuning that got people's attention. Muriel Mussen, who sat in a small office off the showroom floor, came to recognize his tuning when she heard it, for he had an unmistakable, spare style. Most tuners give each key a sharp, forceful blow—called a "test blow"—in order to settle the string and equalize tension. To anyone in close proximity, the test blows can be very loud. Edquist kept his touch gentle, careful not to hit the key any harder than he had to. Halfway into a piano, he would often hear Mussen call out, "I know it's you tuning out there, Verne." That pleased Edquist, who liked to think that his tuning was indeed distinctive, that he took each instrument beyond mere sound and into the realm of color. And he liked to think he offered people a glimpse of that color every time he tuned a piano. Since leaving the School for the Blind, he had spent more than ten years giving one tuning to thousands of pianos. He had little inkling that before long he would spend many more years giving thousands of tunings to just one.

THREE

Astoria

During World War II, Steinway & Sons was directed to put pianos aside and make troop-carrying aircraft. This photograph from 1943 shows workers in the factory putting together the tail assembly for the CG-4A glider. Courtesy of LaGuardia and Wagner Archives.

The piano being the kind of beast it is, it's largely an instrument that is imaginative. In fact, nothing, really, should work in the piano at all. I mean, you have a bunch of materials that are largely incongruous—materials that really don't fit with one another—iron and wood and felt. These are all materials that are essentially in conflict with one another and, of course, this Western imagination has created an illusion that they are perfectly harmonious.

—David Rubin, manager, Concert and
Artists department, Steinway & Sons

In 1942, when Verne Edquist was eleven years old and had yet to learn the rudiments of piano tuning at the Ontario School for the Blind, and as ten-year-old Glenn Gould was starting his studies at the Toronto Conservatory, a piano both men would grow intimately familiar with was being built in fits and starts five hundred miles to the south in Astoria, Queens.

That this collection of wood, wire, metal, and glue eventually became an elegant and ravishing ebony beauty was something close to a miracle, as it was built during the period just after America entered World War II, when the government began to commandeer factories of all kinds for the war effort: Steinway & Sons was directed by the government to build components for combat gliders. It was an extraordinary request. Not only was Steinway & Sons unaccustomed to adapting to new routines, especially those it hadn't invented itself, but by the 1940s it was making the world's finest musical instruments. To be asked now to switch over to mass-producing wooden airplane parts required a seismic shift in the corporate mind-set. And it was a mind-set that had been fixed in bedrock a century earlier.

IN 1836, HEINRICH Engelhard Steinweg, a cabinetmaker by trade, cobbled together a piano in the kitchen of his home in the town of Seesen, Germany. From then on, what set Steinway & Sons apart was a combination of rigor, wile, and inventive risk.

Steinweg's first bold move, in 1850, was to sell a prospering piano company, uproot himself and his family, and, at the age of fifty-three, sail to America. He took most of his children with him, leaving the eldest, C. F. Theodore, behind to run what little remained of the family business. Many years later, family members guessed that the reason for the wholesale move to America was purely economic: Germany was in a recession, a rigid tariff structure was bogging business down, and the free-enterprise promise of America was too enticing to resist.

The first thing the Steinwegs did when they arrived in New York was fan out across the city. Although the Steinwegs had already been running a productive factory in Germany for some years, in order to learn about American manufacturing techniques Heinrich and his sons took jobs at different piano factories in New York. And they had plenty to choose from: Every major city on the Eastern Seaboard could claim at least a few piano makers. In New York alone there were nearly two dozen. Charles and William worked for William Nunns & Co., a prominent piano maker whose instruments were known for their high-quality cabinetry. Henry Junior went to work for James Pirsson, who had invented a double piano that was not unlike a tandem bicycle. And Heinrich made soundboards for a manufacturer named Leuchte, earning six dollars a week. (Had he bothered to learn English and worked for an American, he could have earned double that.) Piano building was evolving in

Europe, but much more slowly than in America. When it came to innovation in piano building, the Steinwegs soon discovered, America was the place to be. It was American piano makers who were changing the way pianos were built, breaking major new ground with plate and action design and stringing techniques. Three years later, in 1853, equipped with an insider's understanding of the process of building a piano in America, the family regrouped, Americanized their name, and formed Steinway & Sons.

The experience had been especially beneficial for Henry Junior, a curious young man who lifted the lid of every piano he saw, looking for new ideas. It was he who introduced an innovation that would eventually be adopted by piano manufacturers around the world, and would ultimately change the way piano music would be heard and played. Henry's idea called for a single cast-iron frame that could hold the 230 heavy-gauge piano wires in tune under tremendous tension—as much as forty-six thousand pounds, or twenty tons. The single metal plate allowed for this much greater string tension, which in turn allowed the use of bigger, heavier—and thus louder—strings that produced a larger, brighter, bolder sound than had been heard in Europe. Moreover, the single plate held the strings in tune for a longer period. With this innovation came bigger sound and bigger concert halls.

It was Henry who was awarded the company's first patents, for improvements to grand piano action. And Henry completely rearranged the way that the strings on a piano had traditionally been placed by innovating an "overstringing" technique in which the bass strings, instead of running parallel to the others, were strung over them diagonally in a second layer. This arrangement allowed for the use of longer strings that were capable of producing greater contrasts between loud and soft as well as a richer, more complex tone. The result was an instrument unlike any heard before. The 350-pound cast-iron plate was the essential innovation that led to Steinway & Sons' rise to the top of the highly competitive business of piano building in the nineteenth century.

The unprecedented stream of innovations ended abruptly with Henry's death in 1865, of tuberculosis, at age thirty-four. "Mr. Steinway had reduced the manufacture of pianofortes to a science," read the brief obituary in the *New York Times*, "and it is probable that few men ever lived who were better acquainted with the construction of the instrument." His brother Charles died a month later, of typhoid fever, at age thirty-six.

Heinrich placed William in charge of the company, and William in turn implored C. F. Theodore, the lone holdout in Germany, to come to New York. While back in Germany, Theodore had designed and built pianos of his own, and when he arrived in the United States in late 1865, he picked up where Henry had left off. Between 1868 and 1885 he was awarded forty-five patents for various aspects of piano design and manufacture. It was when Theodore and William paired up, combining Theodore's engineering genius with William's entrepreneurial skills, that the company began to take off.

William started at Steinway at age eighteen as a "bellyman," installing soundboards, but his legacy would be that of marketing genius. Before the birth of the concert-management industry, Steinway's concert department was actually a production operation that booked performances for pianists. The company did this not because it wanted to but because no one else did it, and Steinway wanted to expose the superiority of the Steinway piano to as wide an audience as possible. So the company set out to get the best pianists of the day to play Steinways before large audiences. In 1860 Henry had come up with the idea of shipping a Steinway grand to Franz Liszt. The plan fizzled, but the Steinway brothers knew that if the company could lure a famous musician to play on a Steinway, it could increase the value of the brand. Around 1870, fighting for recognition among other, better-known piano makers—Chickering, Mason & Hamlin, Baldwin—the company started the "Endorsement Program." The motivation was simple: Since no members of the Steinway family were themselves concert-ready pianists, they reached out to those who were.

In 1872, William broke new ground when he brought Anton Rubinstein, the eminent Russian pianist, to the United States for a 215-concert tour. All the performances, which Rubinstein played over the course of a grueling 239 days, were on Steinways. The company kept six pianos in constant rail transit to accommodate each of the concerts, and a Steinway technician traveled with each piano to keep it tuned and regulated.

William also carried out an intensive brand-awareness campaign. He solicited letters from well-known musicians including Berlioz, Wagner, and Saint-Saëns to provide testimonials to the perfection of the Steinway piano. He was a pioneer in using newspaper advertisements to promote a product, and ultimately succeeded in convincing an entire tier of American society that unless a girl could play the piano, she wasn't likely to get far in life. William pried the piano from its roots as an amusement for the idle wealthy and replanted it as a mark of respectability for all households. William likewise pioneered the idea early on of building a network of dealers who were given exclusive rights to sell Steinway pianos. Every dealer in a major city maintained a "piano bank" of concert grands for touring Steinway artists to choose from.

In 1864, the company opened an elegant showroom next to Union Square on East Fourteenth Street in Manhattan. Two years later, directly behind the store, the company inaugurated Steinway Hall, a two-thousand-seat theater, which went on to become the city's cultural center and home to the New York

Philharmonic until Carnegie Hall opened in 1891. Steinway Hall was much more than a concert hall: It was a brilliant marketing device that took concertgoers to their destination only after they had passed through the ornate, white-marble showroom filled with square, upright, and grand pianos. The main showroom remained at Union Square until 1925, when a new, still more elaborate sales headquarters opened on West Fifty-seventh Street, with a more modest concert hall on the third floor.

The emphasis on marketing continued long after William's death in 1896. In the early 1900s, the advertising phrase that would come to define Steinway for nearly a century came in a flash to Raymond Rubicam, then a young advertising copywriter. Upon learning that a Steinway piano had been used by nearly every great pianist and most of the great composers since Wagner, Rubicam scribbled the words "The Instrument of the Immortals" on a notepad. And in a series of national advertisements, he linked the phrase with portraits of great pianists: Rubinstein, Hofmann, Rachmaninoff. Throughout the early part of the twentieth century, even at times when the overall production of pianos decreased, that one line helped propel the steady rise of Steinway & Sons. And the phrase "The Instrument of the Immortals" eventually took its place alongside other famous advertising slogans like "Breakfast of Champions" and "I'd Walk a Mile for a Camel."

William's son Theodore took over the company in 1927, and had the misfortune of presiding over it when the Great Depression hit. Theodore was not much of a businessman to begin with, and the mid-1930s were the worst years in the history of the company, as it was beset not just by the general economic downturn but by radio's rise in popularity. Piano manufacturing in general fell sharply, and dozens of firms failed. At Steinway & Sons, sales were so dismal that the factory was nearly shut down. Running the company during those years all but killed Theodore: He drank heavily and developed a multitude of health problems.

It was into this state of affairs in 1937, around the time that Glenn Gould was getting his first piano lessons from his mother, that Theodore's son Henry Z. wandered into the family business. The affable and pragmatic twenty-two-year-old was the great-grandson of Henry Engelhard Steinway, the founder, and grandson of William, the marketing genius. He returned to New York after graduating from Harvard, with no clear prospects for a career. After a summer of lazing about, he told an interviewer years later, he thought to himself, "Well, what the hell, I'll try Steinway for a while." He entered an apprenticeship program for young Steinways that sent him from department to department over the course of a few years, earning the Depression-era minimum wage of ten dollars a week. By the end of his first year he had acquired a working knowledge of every facet of piano construction.

Henry was certainly no craftsman; as an apprentice, it took him a full week to build the same case that a seasoned Steinway workman would make in eight hours. And he was definitely no artist. Of course, he had taken piano lessons starting at age six, as his father fervently believed that if you were a Steinway, you should play the piano. Theodore played, as did every other Steinway in his generation, and he raised his children to believe they were part of something special—"this whole piano thing," as Henry Z. once described it. But he hated practicing and knew that his talents lay elsewhere. He was an intuitive businessman and took quickly to the rhythms of the business: sales, lumber procurement, factory administration, and relations with Steinway dealers and pianists. And he showed a particular talent for labor relations. It was Henry Z. who would come to guide the company through the second half of the twentieth century, a time of retrenchment and renewed postwar growth. And it was he who would make the acquaintance of Glenn Gould, and in the process navigate his way through one of the company's most difficult partnerships with any artist in its long history.

No sooner had Henry Z. begun his corporate ascent than new setbacks befell the company. World War II brought havoc to Steinway & Sons. In 1942, the War Production Board, which regulated "nonessential" industrial activities, restricted piano manufacturers' production of new instruments. And recognizing the potential that piano factories offered for necessary war work, the government conscripted the piano industry to build aircraft parts. A scarcity of metal made wood the centerpiece of airplane design. With its piano production shut down, Steinway & Sons leased one of its factory buildings to an aircraft maker that manufactured a troop-carrying combat glider called the CG-4A. Steinway & Sons signed on as subcontractor for the woodwork. Stacks of spruce that Steinway had carefully selected for its soundboards were used instead to make parts for the CG-4A: the wings, underbodies, and tail assemblies, as well as the nose, where the pilot sat, and the benches for the crews. In the process, the company had to move the pianos and other inventory out to an annex to make room for the glider parts. And where Steinway workers had once been artisans bending layered strips of maple into the elegant arch of a grand piano, they were now carving huge sheets of plywood into wings for a mammoth glider designed to carry combat-ready troops silently across enemy lines.

Indeed, in 1942, as America built momentum with its manufacturing might, factories across the country were ordered to stop making vacuum cleaners and washing machines and instead manufacture gun turrets and canteens. Still, it was one thing to convert a home-appliance factory and quite another to commandeer a piano manufacturer—especially if that piano

manufacturer was Steinway & Sons, which for the past nine decades had been producing exquisite musical instruments.
Steinway workers felt a distinct sense of calling, and they considered themselves members of a rarefied community. Workers
in the Steinway factory, even those without an ounce of musical
talent, would say that it was easy to get hooked on pianos. Even
after spending all day at the factory making pianos for as little as
seventy-five cents an hour, they would go home and talk pianos
with their families. This was especially true in families with
more than one generation at the plant.

The Astoria factory was home to more than a thousand
workers—men who were too old for the army, and immigrants
from Italy, Ireland, and Germany. In fact, there were so many
German workers that for a time German was the predominant
language heard inside the factory. Many of them had been at
Steinway for decades, and most lived within a few blocks of one
another. By Christmas of 1942 they were building glider components, and as the tasks changed, the face of the workforce
changed as well. Hundreds of women were brought in, and the
factory had to be reconfigured with new bathrooms because until then the Steinway & Sons workforce had been exclusively
male.

The gliders, it turned out, were nose-heavy and not altogether airworthy, not because they were poorly manufactured
but because they were poorly designed. The huge all-purpose
wooden boxes the gliders were shipped in ended up being more
useful than the planes: Henry Z. Steinway later heard the story
of a military unit that received a shipment of gliders, took them
out of their crates, burned the planes, and slept in the crates.
But it wasn't only gliders that distracted Steinway's workers during the war years. Soon after the government finally ended its
aircraft program, and in an effort to get the company through
the aftereffects of the Depression years, Steinway & Sons turned

to making an item that was increasingly in demand: caskets. Its workers and technicians churned out a full range of coffins made from some of the choicest wood that was stored in the Steinway lumberyards, hundreds of thousands of feet of spruce, maple, walnut, poplar, and mahogany.

It was in the fog of those lost years during World War II that CD 318, the piano that Glenn Gould would one day come to cherish, came into being. Piano production had not been completely halted during the war years. Steinway was given permission to make a thousand or so vertical pianos, the solid, war-rugged, homely, and practical forty-inch instruments that came to be called "G.I. uprights." Those pianos, some painted olive drab, others gray, were designed with a simple, heavy block case. They were shipped out in special packing containers to military bases, many of them overseas, along with instruction manuals and tuning tools in the unlikely event that there was a soldier who knew how to use them. And other pianos, already in the works when Pearl Harbor was attacked in December 1941, managed to inch along to completion.

The piano that would eventually become CD 318 started out as W 905, a factory designation it most likely received when the rim was first bent to form the distinctive outline of a concert grand. Since a piano moves through a factory for many months before receiving its serial number, there needed to be a means of marking a piano while it was still under construction. For that purpose, Steinway & Sons used letters, cycling through the alphabet on a regular basis. W had first come around in 1897, was used again in 1918, and now returned in 1942 when work commenced on the 905th piano of the year. Surely it was part of the piano's improbable fate that work on it began when it did, because its construction began just before the piano-making prohibition went into effect.

Even in the best of times, building a concert grand is a slow process, although workers at Steinway were never idle. If they stopped working on one piano because it was waiting for glue to dry or for lacquer to cure, they started on another. Over the years Steinway's concert grands had become a particular source of pride for the company. The Steinway Model D, as it is recognized today, was first conceived by C. F. Theodore Steinway in 1883. The first such piano, with a rosewood case, was finished in 1884 and sold to a man named M. D. Stevens of New York in June 1885. Each Model D that emerged from the factory thereafter was a masterpiece of thousands of separate parts that were glued, pressed, planed, machined, hammered, and screwed into place. Workers marveled (and complained) that a concert grand Model D's twelve thousand parts—D for damn big, they'd commonly say—felt more like fifty thousand.

The process of manufacturing a piano like W 905 had changed little in the nearly one hundred years since Henry Steinway started the company. Despite a few advances in manufacturing techniques, in the 1940s the creation of a grand piano was as labor-intensive as it ever had been. The multitude of parts and processes required the involvement of some 250 workers, including specialists in mechanical engineering, design, carpentry, cabinetmaking, wood finishing, metallurgy, tuning, and voicing. The plate department ran on steam power and elbow grease, and the soundboards were shaped by careful craftsmen who used hand planes, chisels, mallets, saws, and calipers. The individual handcrafting of each piano remains a source of great pride to Steinway even as it has witnessed the success Yamaha enjoys with its assembly-line process. Eventually, in the 1970s, Henry Z. gave credit to the Japanese for helping to boost sales of modern grand pianos by bringing large quantities of them into the country. But the tradition at Steinway, which carried into the late twentieth century, was to value handwork and individual craftsmanship, and to make the workers feel that they were part of a brotherhood of craftsmen as well as members of the Steinway family.

Joe and Ralph Bisceglie, brothers who both worked at Steinway for nearly four decades, typified the tradition of loyalty and longevity among Steinway's factory workers. It was workers like the Bisceglie brothers that Henry Z. knew he could depend on for consistency and craftsmanship—Astoria boys whose parents had come from Italy through Ellis Island, who started at Steinway after high school and never left. Employees like the Biseglies knew that if you worked at Steinway long enough and hard enough, Henry Z. took care of you. "Even if you got in trouble with Steinway and he fired you, it was like a slap on the wrist . . . and he hired you back," said Joe Bisceglie, who eventually rose to the level of senior factory technician. "We had guys hired fifteen different times after they were let go. Because I guess even Steinway himself realized, where would you go? If you worked on pianos all your life, where else could you go?"

Most of Steinway's craftsmen took enormous pride in the work they did. Many, from the tone regulators to the bellymen, signed their names and the date somewhere inside each piano they worked on, especially the concert grands. Often the signatures would be made in pencil on the side of the lowest A, the first key on the piano. And sometimes a worker signed his name so far inside the piano that it would never be seen unless the instrument was taken apart for repair. A factory worker once recounted the story of walking past an old man, a second- or third-generation factory employee, weeping as he repaired an old piano. He had found the signature of his father—then dead for forty years—inscribed deep inside the instrument.

For all its manufacturing rigor, Steinway & Sons never produced a formal blueprint for building its first Model D. Henry and C. F. Theodore made a few scale drawings, but for the most part, instead of a piano being built from blueprints or any other sort of written instructions, the specifications were handed down from each generation of craftsmen to the next, over many decades of building pianos. They were simply built, then refined; then more were built. Throughout the years, each foreman carried a small notebook in his back pocket and wrote down every detail of how things were done. In this way, the specifications, such as they were, were passed down from foreman to foreman.

To Henry Z., in the business of piano making, craft came before science. General Motors had hundreds of engineers who made detailed drawings of every screw that went into a car before a model went into production. "In the piano business it works the other way around," he once observed. "You start with a piano and say, oh, we'll make this here . . . make this plate a little longer here . . . move this one inch, and so on." So it was that W 905 evolved.

Under normal circumstances, producing a Steinway concert grand like W 905 could take the better part of a year. Add to that the preproduction process and it could be more like two years. The moisture-laden lumber, some of it containing up to 80 percent water, has to be dried, first out in the air and then in a kiln, for anywhere from nine months to five years depending on where in the piano the wood is going. Work can't begin until the moisture content falls to around 6 percent. The drier the wood, the less likely it is to change dimensions after being installed in a piano. Steinway has always spent a great deal of money on its wood, yet fully half of the dried lumber is rejected because it has an imperfection, like a knot or an uneven grain pattern, which are the marks of a weaker spot in the wood.

One unique aspect of piano construction that Steinway patented and is still in use today is the building of the piano's inner and outer rims, which give a grand its sensual curves.

Eighteen rock-hard layers of maple, each twenty-two feet long and still fairly moist so it can be forced into one sinewy shape, are first coated with glue and stacked into layers; then glued into a single form of wood and wrestled onto a giant, gracefully curved, piano-shaped vise; locked into place with clamps; then put in a darkened, climate-controlled "rim-bending" room and cured for several weeks.

As the rim is curing and the wood is growing accustomed to its new shape, other parts are being built, including the soundboard, the acoustical centerpiece of the instrument. The soundboard serves the essential purpose of amplifying the sound that's created when a hammer hits a slender string, making it capable of reverberating through a huge concert hall. The soundboard is a large wooden diaphragm with a long strip of laminated maple called the bridge, which is much like the bridge on a violin, running from one side to the other. Over that bridge, at high tension, are stretched more than two hundred strings that constitute the tone-generating element of the piano. When the piano is played, the strings pass over the bridge, which transfers the energy into the soundboard, which in turn repeats the vibratory motions of the strings and sets in vibration much more air than the strings would on their own, thus intensifying the sound. The more faithfully a soundboard performs this function, the better its quality. On a Model D like W 905, the soundboard was built to withstand the combined downward force of nearly one thousand pounds. W 905's soundboard was made of close-grained quarter-sawn spruce, a lightweight yet strong wood that is considered the very best—some would say the only—wood for soundboards because its long parallel fibers make it flexible enough to vibrate freely and project sound while remaining strong enough to support the weight of the piano's strings. The soundboard panel is composed of approximately twenty boards that are glued together along their lengths and bow out slightly in the center. First the ribs—long, narrow strips of spruce—are glued to the underside of the soundboard so that the board is distorted into a slight crown, which increases its ability to project sound waves into the air. Then the bridge is doweled and glued to the top of the soundboard. The factory workers, of course, were constructing piano W 905 for a ghost. No one could have imagined that the musician who would eventually fall in love with this specific piano was at the time a ten-year-old boy living in Toronto who was already particular to the point of obsession, not just about the music he would play but about the instrument he would play it on. They couldn't know that this child possessed a sense of touch so uncannily sensitive that he could feel the tiniest bit of unevenness in the action. And those Steinway factory workers in the early 1940s had no way of knowing that the main appeal of W 905 would, for this extremely tactile young musician up in Toronto, lie in its action.

The action on a modern grand is a marvelously complex device. A self-contained mechanism that includes not just the keyboard but all the levers and hammers behind the keys, the action translates the downward pressure of the finger on the key to the corresponding hammer, propelling the hammer to strike the strings. The action is composed of felt, leather, spring wire, wood, and small pieces of metal, which work together to accomplish an array of different functions simultaneously. The action not only sets the hammers in motion but, because it is a lever mechanism, it is able to do so in a way that makes the hammers move farther and faster than the keys do in order to reach the strings. Once a key is depressed, it is the action's job to see to it that the hammer travels independently over the last fraction of its path and rebounds immediately after striking the strings, even if the key is still depressed. Simultaneously, the dampers—pieces of felt glued to a small block of wood resting above the string—are sent into motion, preventing the strings from unintentionally vibrating once the key has been released. As if that wasn't enough to worry about, the overeager hammer must be prevented from bouncing back up to the strings as a result of its own momentum. At the same time, the action has to allow for the fact that the pianist might want to restrike a note without having to lift his finger entirely off the key, so the part that propels the hammer—called a jack—must return to its original position, ready to strike again. Meanwhile, the damper that has been sitting over the strings, preventing them from vibrating, must rise so the strings can sound cleanly, but must fall back promptly to cut off the sound when the key is released.

Steinway didn't invent the piano action. That was the work of Bartolomeo Cristofori in the early 1700s. Cristofori is often credited with inventing the modern piano as we know it, and Cristofori's main achievement was inventing the action. Before the eighteenth century, stringed keyboard instruments were extremely limited in terms of how the strings could be made to vibrate. On a harpsichord, strings are plucked by a quill, which produces the same volume no matter how firmly the key is struck. On a clavichord—another early keyboard instrument that was in use during the fifteenth century—the strings were struck with a small metal blade that was embedded in the back of each key. The musician could control the volume of individual notes, but there wasn't much volume to control: As soon as the clavichordist removed his finger from the key, the sound would evaporate.

Cristofori's innovation was to build an instrument that he described as an *arpicembalo che fa il piano e il forte*, a harpsichord that plays soft and loud. It was eventually shortened to *pianoforte*. Cristofori's instrument was exceptionally sophisticated. Instead of using quills to pluck the strings, tiny leather-covered hammers struck them head-on. Cristofori's invention also contained a rudimentary escapement mechanism that let the hammers fall away quickly. In fact, the fifty-four keys on Cristofori's pianoforte performed all the functions of a modern piano with one exception: the "repetition," which allows a note to be restruck before the key returns to its original position. This shortcoming was eventually corrected in the early 1800s by a French piano maker, Sebastien Erard, who came up with what is called the double-escapement mechanism, which permitted a note to be repeated even if the pianist's finger had not yet fully released the key. The double escapement eventually became the standard action on grand pianos, employed by every manufacturer, including, of course, Steinway & Sons.

Because piano actions are so complex, many piano makers didn't bother to build their own, and instead would buy the action from an outside supplier. But Steinway, with its long tradition of craftsmanship, would never stoop to outsourcing. The actions for all of Steinway's grands—including the hammers—were created in the New York factory.

Recognizing that a pianist can give full expression to a piece only if there exists a proper harmony between the pianist and the keyboard, many Steinway workers still regard assembling the action as one of the most rewarding aspects of building a piano. A professional pianist is likely to care most about the piano's action, because that is what controls its responsiveness and relative lightness—or heaviness—of touch. Roughly speaking, a piano's action is light when its keys fall easily under the fingers, and heavy when a noticeable downward thrust is required. The action, in short, is what makes a piano playable or not to an individual musician. Steinway's workers were constantly reminded of this when famous artists came through the factory to play pianos that were just being finished, to see which ones "spoke to their fingers." And it was frequently the action that determined that outcome.

While its action was being built, W 905 underwent belly work, finishing, and stringing. Bellying is one of many custom-fitting operations in the manufacture of a piano, involving the precise and careful joining of the soundboard, the cast-iron plate, and the rim. After that process the soundboard assembly is affixed to the rim. Borrowed, perhaps, from the vernacular of the violin maker, the term *belly* refers to the shape of the sound-board and the bridges and rim that surround it. To some histori-ans, the rounded shape of the violin and piano soundboards resembles a belly. But anyone who watches a bellyman do his job can see immediately where the process gets its name, as a bellyman must lie on his stomach on top of the soundboard to do his work, all the while teetering on the rim of the piano.

After the belly work was finished, W 905 was strung and then chipped, or given its first rough tuning, the first job Verne Edquist had when he started doing factory work. Then the ac-tion and the keyboard were installed. Next came the final pro-cess to the finish, done by the rubbing department: a pumice stone and oil are rubbed on the lacquered case parts to remove the rough coating and give the piano a satin finish.

Like many pianos built during the war, W 905 kept getting delayed. Work was done in the hours that could be captured be-tween the manufacture of glider parts, packing crates, helicop-ter floors, rifle stocks, and army-issue uprights. Piano parts often lay scattered around the factory until someone was free to assemble them.

Finally W 905's action was pieced together, and the piano un-derwent the action and tone regulating that would bring its mechanism and sound to their peak. Regulating the action re-quires the technician to delicately and precisely adjust the thou-sand or so moving parts in the keyboard mechanism in order to ensure maximum evenness for the pianist, which in turn trans-lates to maximum control. If a pianist is struggling against an uneven action, it hampers his ability to phrase a piece just as he wants it.

The process of fine-tuning W 905's action entailed fitting the keys, hammers, and dampers into the newly strung piano, and making sure that the hammer rebounded instantly after coming into contact with the strings so that the strings had ample opportunity to vibrate for as long as the key was held down. Each hammer on W 905 was made to rise and hit the three strings squarely, and the keys were then leveled. The damper felts were matched to the strings, and the levers that controlled each of the dampers were adjusted. Finally, the technician adjusted the spring tension and aligned the many small parts for each note. In a process called the action weigh-off, every key was then calibrated so that they all would have a consistent feel. The technician placed brass weights on each key, meant to simulate the downward pressure of a pianist's finger, and then inserted lead underneath each key covering until the pressure needed to depress a key was the same across the entire span of eighty-eight keys. When he was done, every key would contain varying amounts of lead, but each would fall with approximately fifty grams of downward pressure.

Then came the instrument's tone. Compared to the rich resonance of a finished piano, an instrument that is still under construction sounds terrible. Some notes buzz while others fade too fast, and they don't project the way they should—they don't seem loud enough. This is where the tone regulator comes in. His job is to transform a piano from a mass of moving parts into a musical instrument with the complexity, beauty, and magic of a Steinway grand.

Tone regulating—the term was later gussied up and changed to "voicing"—was a coveted job at Steinway. Workers strove, and were indeed encouraged, to progress from the physical labor of case, rim, and belly work—to say nothing of the noxious fumes from the glue—to the more nuanced work that involved making the instrument more musical. Voicing a piano in the final stages of construction, after the action weigh-off, is a simple process with complex repercussions. It has nothing to do with tuning—although most voicers have received training in tuning—and everything to do with the quality of sound and the evenness of volume that is produced by each note. It is perhaps the most subjective part of the piano-building process, performed by a technician with well-trained ears and hands. Voicing requires that the technician subtly alter the texture of the hammer felt (each hammer in a piano is covered with one or two layers of compressed wool felt), which is critical to forming each piano's distinctive sound and personality. A voicer makes adjustments to the hammer's resiliency by driving a small row of needles into its felt. This separates the fibers and makes the tone mellower, rounder, or more open. Needling the felt on certain parts of the hammer can even make the tone stronger and louder. The ultimate goal of voicing is to give a pianist access to the widest possible dynamic range—from the softest, creamiest whisper to a brassy, hard-edged, crashing fortissimo—all emanating from the same hammer. Like a skilled acupuncturist, a master voicer knows how to get these different effects through either shallow or deep needling of the felt, or, if he wants to increase the brilliance of a note, by applying lacquer to it. It is a delicate process: Overneedling or overlacquering can ruin a set of hammers, and in turn the tone of the piano.

It is the voicer who ensures that the piano's sound is as powerful as it can be without destroying its capacity for softness and warmth. The process can take several days. As Ralph Bisceglie explained, "You're working with eighty-eight notes and you've got to do the same operations on each one." And overnight, after a full day of meticulous needling, everything changes with the small heaves and sighs of the wood.

Any technician knows that a bad voicing job can ruin a set of hammers, but there is also great pride to be had in voicing—because it is in the voicing that a piano maker can have a real influence on the instrument. Voicing gave employees who loved music a chance to indulge their passion, allowing them to impose a little of their own musicality on a piano. The sound of a piano can vary dramatically, depending on what the voicer has done. A piano voiced in a mellow tone for the music room of a typical home, for instance, can be swallowed up in a concert hall. And what one person might perceive as mellow, another might hear as weak. This subjectivity—this unquantifiable sense that guides the essential voicing process—is part of what makes each piano distinct, while at the same time it is what creates the characteristic "Steinway sound."

Although every Steinway was made the same way, from the same materials and by the same workers to the same specifications, each piano that emerged from the factory, mysteriously enough, felt and sounded different. Some ended up sounding small or mellow, fine for chamber music. Some were so percussive that a full-strength orchestra could not drown them out. On some, the keys moved almost effortlessly. On others the pianist's hands and arms got a workout. W 905 ended up with an exceptionally light touch, an action so delicate it would eventually attract the attention of the highly demanding Glenn Gould.

W 905 was actually a twin. When work started on Glenn Gould's future piano, construction on another concert grand—W 902—had already begun. As was often the case with Model D's, the pianos would travel through the manufacturing process together. Both ended up as especially fine instruments—which could have been due to the crew of artisans that put them together, so starved for concert pianos to build as they spent the war years on the relatively artless work of airplane parts. Perhaps they lavished their finest craftsmanship on those two pianos. But something else set W 905 apart that might have had more to do with the materials that went into it. Perhaps it was the wood that gave the piano its personality. No matter how carefully Steinway workers selected or prepared each batch of lumber, it's a fact that in the forest, some trees get more sunlight than others, and some get more moisture. Perhaps the trees that became W 905 received more sunlight, giving the wood more resonance. Or maybe it was the quality of that particular batch of hammer felt. Steinway used a yellow-tinted wool that was thicker and more refined than conventional felt. As with everything else in a piano, the quality of the wool affects the tone. For years the wool used for Steinway pianos came from South African merino sheep, known for producing wool fiber that in turn produced dense felt that was also highly resilient, the best combination for hammer felt. Makers of this high-quality felt tried to avoid fibers that came from the underside of the sheep, because although they were longer and technically more desirable, those fibers also carried a higher urine content. But who can say whether that was the felt that was used on W 905? During World War II, like so many other materials basic to piano manufacturing, felt was scarce. For all anyone knows, the felt for W 905 could have been pieced together from scraps.

And who could say what effect the unpredictable, out-of-rhythm construction process of the war years had on both W 905 and W 902? Both pianos were officially declared finished on the same day: March 30, 1943. Yet as the war dragged on, they entered a protracted state of limbo. When Steinway & Sons moved its partly finished pianos out of the factory and into a warehouse to make way for glider parts, the pianos must certainly have been moved as well. No doubt they were then neglected for many months. And they weren't the only instruments to be affected by the on-again, off-again business of piano manufacturing during wartime. In all of 1944, only one concert grand was shipped from the Astoria factory, in contrast to a pre-war high of sixty-three in 1929. In 1945, W 905 was one of ten concert grands to leave the factory, having been given the serial number 317194. This number did not signify that W 905 was necessarily the 317,194th piano built, but that it was the 317,194th piano to be assigned a serial number. W 902 got the serial number 317193. The number 317195 was assigned to one of the wartime pianos, a forty-inch, olive-drab upright that was shipped out to an officers' mess in Kansas.

When the two pianos finally emerged from the Steinway factory in Astoria in 1945, it was against all odds. By early 1945, having managed to end up as pianos and not glider parts or, worse, caskets, W 902 and W 905 were both taken off the showroom floor and selected for service as part of the Concert and Artists fleet. This was a relatively easy decision, because there were fewer pianos to choose from. The Steinway & Sons logo above the keyboard, which included the company's famous lyre, was replaced by larger letters that read, simply, STEINWAY. Finally, the two nine-foot grands, relatively anonymous behemoths up to now, were officially assigned their CD designations: 317 and 318. CD 317 would end up staying at Steinway & Sons on Fifty-seventh Street for twelve more years before it was sold in 1957—and moved just a block away—to Helen Hobbs Jordan, the famous music teacher who lived next door to Carnegie Hall. CD 318 spent approximately a year at Steinway & Sons before it was crated up, loaded onto a train, and shipped to the T. Eaton Company in Toronto, where it was placed in the company's small fleet of pianos that were reserved for professional concerts and recitals.

Unlike some pianos that become instant favorites, no one singled out CD 318 as an exceptional instrument; its hidden virtues and native inclinations would eventually be teased out, over a period of many years, by the right combination of pianist and technician. As it was played by touring concert artists, CD 318's hammer felt gradually wore down and required periodic reshaping or softening, and the parts of its action required continual adjustment and readjustment. Joe Bisceglie, who would one day, many years later, find himself face to face with Glenn Gould's piano when it was in dire need of repair, compares a concert-grand piano to a finely tuned racing engine: There's a point at which it's ready to run flat out, and only the constant attention of a master mechanic can keep it there. For CD 318, that genius would turn out to be Verne Edquist.

FOUR

The Trouble with Pianos

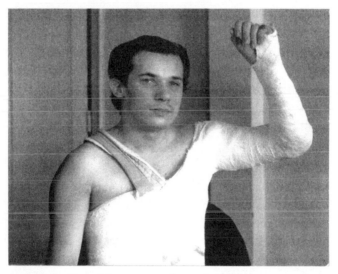

In 1960, Gould sued Steinway & Sons after an enthusiastic pat on the shoulder from Bill Hupfer, Steinway's chief technician. At one point, Gould was placed in this extensive cast. Photograph by Adrian Siegel.

*I played well in Pasadena, despite the second-worst piano
I've encountered all year (the worst being my own).*
                    —Glenn Gould in a 1957 letter to a friend

FOR ALL THE YEARS THAT Glenn Gould spent search-
ing for the perfect piano, what he didn't know was that the instrument that would ultimately fulfill every one of his very
particular requirements was sitting right under his nose in
Toronto. Still, his years of seeking would take him to New York
dozens of times, not just to make records but to badger and
goad the managers at Steinway into helping him find the instrument of his dreams. When he wasn't in New York to pester
them in person, he would plead his case in lengthy letters to the
company's executives.

Steinway & Sons liked to consider itself both friend and
counsel to its artists, who had an open invitation to use Steinway Hall as their headquarters whenever they were in New
York, to use the practice rooms for as long as they wished, and
to drop in on members of the Concert and Artists department. By the early twentieth century, more than 95 percent of
piano soloists performing with major orchestras used Steinway pianos exclusively. Aware that they were building extremely important relationships with each and every famous
musician who played their pianos, Steinway's Concert and
Artists executives, many of whom were musicians themselves,
spent a great deal of time and energy cultivating those relationships.

Until the Depression put a stop to the practice, Steinway

artists received free pianos to keep in their homes. Many were also given free practice pianos for their hotel rooms. Part of bending over backward for Steinway artists meant indulging their occasional abuses of the pianos. On one occasion, a hotel piano was returned with a large mark on the lid. It turned out that the pianist had needed a flat surface on which to have his pants ironed. Theodore Steinway, who was president of the company at the time, tried to make light of the damage to such a fine instrument by inviting the pianist to provide a testimonial to the effect that "The Steinway is the finest piano on which to press my pants."

Beyond indulging the sloppy treatment of some of its finest pianos, Steinway also catered to other, frequently unusual demands from its major artists. For Josef Hofmann, Steinway craftsmen built three custom keyboards, with each key slightly narrower than the standard, to accommodate his unusually short fingers. They constructed special chairs for Paderewski and Hofmann and a bench with adjustable feet for Horowitz, who was frequently troubled by the unevenness of the floor on a concert stage.

David Rubin, a vice president who ran the concert department throughout the 1960s and 1970s, described the philosophy that guided Steinway's relationship with its artists. The first mandate is to nurture the relationship and do everything possible to ensure that the artist is happy with Steinway's pianos. The second is more complicated and nuanced, and concerns what he called the "exterior relationship." "I'm convinced that the difference between an artist and an ordinary player has to do with something that goes on inside someone's head," Rubin said. "In terms of the piano itself, there is an aural concept of what the artist, in his imagination, hears, something they are listening for. I try to find out what it is that they're listening for. They show me. I think we are outrageously successful if we measure up to about sixty percent of what an artist is looking for. That's very, very high. Once in a while you'll get to seventy percent. But you'll never get to one hundred percent because what they're experiencing within themselves has to do with imagination and we are dealing with a physical product. And that physical product, in some way, has to coincide—that's about as close as we can get to what they are trying to feel, hear, express, and project."

The main place where Steinway's relationship with its artists was developed was the famous Basement at the company's headquarters and showroom on West Fifty-seventh Street, just off Seventh Avenue and across the street from Carnegie Hall. Many Steinway artists entered the Basement from a lower-level door around the side of the building, but those who made the journey from the first floor took a more scenic route. Entering from Fifty-seventh Street, they would glimpse the domed reception room through a ten-by-fifteen-foot window framed by marble columns on either side. As they passed through the octagonal rotunda, if they looked toward the ceiling they would see handpainted allegorical scenes surrounding a multitiered crystal chandelier. And on their way to the elevators they passed original artwork that included paintings by N. C. Wyeth and Rockwell Kent, set off by green pilasters of highly polished marble. Had they been potential customers, they would have been escorted through a large set of Italian marble pillars to one of the piano selection rooms, or "display salons," decorated with plush drapes and large, comfortable armchairs.

In the Basement, Steinway & Sons dispensed with all such finery. Pianists who went there hoped to be impressed by one thing and one thing only: pianos. The Basement was a cavernous, windowless room with a wide sliding door and a wood floor on which piano-leg casters easily rolled. Of the roughly 150 pianos that normally compose the Steinway lending library, there was always, in the Basement, a cluster of around twenty or so Model D's, the eight-foot-eleven-and-a-quarter-inch concert grands, as well as a few six-foot-eleven-inch Model B's, all in ebonized black, lined up in two rows with their keyboards facing each other, kept in perfect tune and adjustment for whatever visiting artist might be coming through New York for a performance at one of the city's great concert halls.

It was the job of the Concert and Artists department to find the perfect instrument for any pianist's needs. Many factors came into play, including the artist's state of mind on any given day. Rubin recalled the day that Horacio Gutiérrez, then at the beginning of his career, visited the Steinway Basement. The moment Rubin set eyes on him he knew there was something about the way the pianist comported himself that didn't bode well. Indeed, every piano that Gutiérrez played sounded terrible, not just to the pianist but to Rubin as well. Rubin told him to return a few days later and promised to give him a few more pianos to play. When Gutiérrez came back, this time with his wife—"which, in his case, happens to make a great difference," Rubin said—all the pianos, even the ones he had tried a few days earlier that had sounded awful, now sounded wonderful. He chose one of the pianos from the earlier session. Rubin recalled, "Four days earlier, he said, 'Well, none of these pianos have any sound.' And indeed they didn't. And then four days later they all did." Steinway had done nothing except add a few more pianos to choose from. The revelation for Rubin was that even under the best conditions, what constitutes a good piano could change according to a pianist's mood. "It had to do with how he felt, how he woke up that morning," Rubin said. And then there was what Rubin called "that inspirational quality," an inscrutable aspect that cannot be ignored. "Maybe he wanted to play for his wife that day. Or maybe he didn't feel like playing without her. Who knows?"

On another occasion Rubin offered what he knew to be an excellent piano to Vladimir Horowitz, who, after playing the instrument, conceded that while the tone was fine and the action suitably light, he'd never use it. When Rubin asked why, the pianist responded, "Well, for me it lacks bouquet." Ever the diplomat, Rubin acquiesced at once and moved Horowitz along to the next piano. Horowitz was using the terminology of wine, but in this context, Rubin recalled years later, "the issue was what the sound produced in terms of, shall we say, the covering mask"—a particular sonic patina that could be heard regardless of the music being played. The piano Horowitz was seeking needed to have a huge palette for the wide range of music he frequently played, with a great deal of room for nuance and vibrancy of color. The perfectly competent piano Horowitz had rejected simply produced a smaller range.

Rudolf Serkin, on the other hand, once told Rubin he wanted "a big healthy sound," leaving Rubin to figure out what that meant. In contrast to Horowitz, Serkin wasn't a seductive, sensual pianist. His was a more intellectual approach, and he was much more focused on the great Austro-German canon: Bach, Mozart, Beethoven, Schubert, and Brahms. Both Horowitz and Serkin were looking for a sound that in some way reflected what each was hearing in his mind.

Over the years Rubin grew skilled at translating pianists' vaguely expressed notions into an instrument that was well suited to their style and musical tastes. Glenn Gould, however, was a different matter. Neither Rubin nor anyone else in the Concert and Artists department was able to satisfy Gould's requirements. Not long into Gould's association with Steinway, which began in 1954, both pianist and piano maker knew that it was going to be a fractious relationship at best. As far as Steinway was concerned, its concert grands were built to meet the needs of the traditional concert pianist. But the company found it almost impossible to furnish Gould with a piano that satisfied him.

Throughout the 1950s, Gould grew increasingly unhappy with most of the Steinways he sat down to play. They had "a sluggish action," the black keys were too long or too narrow, or the white keys were too wide or too smooth. He intensely disliked the new pianos that were emerging from the Steinway factory, and was distressed that Steinway routinely removed from circulation older pianos that he considered perfectly acceptable. The Steinways that Gould—and many other pianists—preferred were the ones that had been made in the 1920s and 1930s, between the two world wars, a period that many consider Steinway's golden age. This, of course, was more than a little irksome to Steinway, whose credo was, "This year's Steinway is the best ever made."

"He doesn't like our contemporary concert grands," Alexander "Sascha" Greiner, a predecessor to Rubin, noted in a memo about Gould, and "this is of no use and benefit to Steinway & Sons whatever. We are not in the business of promoting and selling Steinway pianos which were made 50 or 100 years ago. Our business is to promote the present product."

In truth, the professional concert pianist was not the individual Steinway & Sons had in mind when the company first started manufacturing pianos. The development of the piano had much more to do with the people who wrote for it than with the people who eventually played it. Steinway designed its pianos for the ever-evolving works of Chopin, Liszt, and the other Romantics, the repertoire that was, in the middle of the nineteenth century, preferred by most concert pianists. By then, piano manufacturers like Steinway were designing increasingly robust instruments because the music being composed demanded it. Franz Liszt himself was notorious for breaking pianos. "After the concert Liszt stands there like a victor on the battlefield," wrote one critic. "Daunted pianos lie around him; torn strings wave like flags of truce; frightened instruments flee into distant corners."

Over the years, Steinway pianos became famous for their ability to project more sound and project it farther, to accommodate the kind of music being composed. Steinway pianos came to be known for the distinctive "Steinway sound" they produced: a growling, dramatic bass with an unusual sustaining power, and a singing, brilliant treble. (The word *brilliant* is often used to describe a piano's sound in the upper register. That is, although some pianists like a creamy, luscious pearl-like tone in the treble, most concert players prefer the aural equivalent of diamonds, with hard edges, sharp and brilliant.)

But Glenn Gould seldom played the Romantics, and even spoke scornfully of the entire nineteenth-century piano repertoire, including Beethoven. He had a passion for Beethoven's early sonatas but considered the composer's middle period—the Appassionata and Waldstein, for example—nothing but "junk" (although he did record most of the composer's major works for piano). Gould could be a fickle critic; he dismissed Mozart's later music as either hedonistic or, at the other extreme, mechanical. "Too many of his works sound like interoffice memos," he once wrote. Yet he was very fond of Mozart's early sonatas, especially those with a Baroque character, and he ended up recording all of them.

He liked Mendelssohn but dismissed most of his piano music. He simply ignored Schubert, while more thoroughly denouncing Liszt, Chopin, and Schumann. Early twentieth-century composers like Ravel and Debussy didn't fare much better. And he detested Bartók and Stravinsky; in 1952, when Gould was nineteen, he filled in a questionnaire for the CBC and placed those two musicians under the heading "Most Over-estimated Modern Composers."

In fact, Gould associated Romantic music with what he deemed a corrupting influence on the concertizing life, because he believed it created a powerful temptation to show off technique, to revel in sonority at the expense of musical substance, and to focus on a small, safe repertoire of familiar, mostly Romantic crowd-pleasers.

One further difference that set Gould at odds with much of the musical world was his philosophy of sound. Gould argued that projection was far less crucial than clarity. He wanted to get a dry, clean, light tone from a piano. For example, he adored the spare, reserved music of Orlando Gibbons, a sixteenth-century Tudor composer whom he often called his favorite. It was not Beethoven, Mozart, or Chopin but Gibbons who elicited what Gould called "a very precise—and yet impossible to define—spiritual response from me."

The result, to the dismay and eternal frustration of Steinway's executives, was that Gould largely avoided the music that most fully showcases the piano in general, and Steinway pianos in particular.

This created a paradox, one that would become a leitmotif throughout Gould's life. Though a consummately gifted pianist, he frequently made it clear to friends, technicians, interviewers, and Steinway employees that he did not really care much for the piano as an instrument. For Gould, the making of music was more mental than physical, and it transcended the physical limitations of any instrument—in his case, the piano, which mediated the struggle between music as it was played and music as it might exist in the mind. "You know, the piano is not an instrument for which I have any great love as such," he once told a reporter. But, he added, "I have played it all my life and it's the best vehicle I have to express my ideas."

If Gould idolized anyone, it was Artur Schnabel, the Austrian pianist whose recordings of Beethoven's Fourth Piano Concerto and sonatas Gould did not merely admire but would occasionally imitate in his own performances. Gould's reverence was perhaps less for Schnabel the pianist than for Schnabel the idealist, who seemed to view the piano simply as a means to an end. Schnabel made his mark on the musical world by rejecting technical bravura in favor of musical idealism. When others were showing off their virtuosity with the splashy music of Liszt, Schnabel was busy championing the sonatas of Beethoven and Schubert. As Schnabel himself once put it, "In his endeavor to satisfy the technical demands of the instrument [the musician] can easily neglect the creative task, to the extent of obliterating the imaginative side of the music, for which even the quintessence of dexterity and an infallible apparatus cannot serve as substitutes."

While Gould may have downplayed his affection for the piano as an instrument, he was still hell-bent on finding the perfect Steinway, or "infallible apparatus," in Schnabel's phrase. And Steinway, for its part, did everything it could to appease him.

THOSE WHO INHABIT the world of concert pianos refer to Steinway's concert grands the way railway conductors talk about trains: by the identifying numbers—50, 400, 239, or 15— preceded by the CD designation that signifies that they were part of the elite concert fleet.

Most famous Steinway artists have their favorites. For years, Gary Graffman was enchanted by CD 199, a piano with an extremely long-lasting tone and a huge range of sound that he found less percussive than other Steinways. Graffman frequently extolled the remarkable properties of CD 199 and traveled with it as often as he could. For a time in the 1950s, he and three other young concert pianists grew so attached to CD 199 that they hatched a complicated scheme for shipping the piano around the country for their most important concerts, sharing the transportation costs.

CD 15, long a regular in the Steinway Basement, was a legendary favorite of Rachmaninoff's. Steinway employees were not supposed to admit that one piano might actually differ from another, but they universally conceded that this piano possessed an especially mellow quality. CD 15 developed such a reputation among touring pianists that they tended to ascribe it magical powers, as if the piano were capable of banging out the famous "Rach 3" on its own.

In response to people's tendency to fetishize pianos, Steinway began to assign the CD numbers completely at random. In Steinway's early years, the concert grands in the Basement and the pianos that were sent out to dealers around the country were identified by the first three digits of their serial number. But that gave pianists an approximate idea of a piano's age, and when touring pianists couldn't find a better reason to pick a particular piano, they often selected the newest one, a practice that tended to overwork those pianos while shortchanging perfectly good older instruments. So that system was scrapped and Steinway started assigning CD numbers instead. The CD numbers, which were more like nicknames, signified nothing at all.

The entire Steinway staff colluded to keep the CD designation completely ephemeral. When a concert grand came in for repairs, then was shipped out to another dealer or placed in the Steinway Basement for selection by visiting concert pianists, managers in the Concert and Artists department often intentionally switched its CD number. "It was purposely confusing," said Henry Z. "We didn't want the pianists to get a fetish about a certain number on a piano. So we kept reassigning them. People would come in and say, 'Oh, what happened to good old CD 265?' and chances were pretty good that CD 265 was now CD 175."

Once, following a concert in Worcester, Massachusetts, a pianist complained to Steinway about the miserable qualities of the piano the local dealer had supplied, and the instrument was shipped back to New York. Steinway technicians examined it but did nothing except change the CD number; it was then installed in the Basement. When the pianist showed up in New York a few weeks later to pick out a piano for his next concert, he selected the very same instrument after extolling its "superior tone and touch." But Glenn Gould, with his hyperdiscerning hands, could never be fooled in such a way.

DESPITE THE FRICTION with the idiosyncratic young performer, Steinway labored to satisfy Gould, and through the latter part of the 1950s, in addition to providing pianos for him all over North America, the company also serviced his European concerts and sent concert grands to his hotel rooms around the world.

In 1955 many problems seemed solved when, in a serendipitous moment one day in the Steinway Basement, he discovered CD 174, a concert grand built in 1928. In the course of his unending search for the perfect instrument, Gould had visited the Basement many times, but he and this piano had been like ships in the night. As far as he knew, it had never been there when he was.

Gould was convinced that he needed wider gaps between the white keys so that he could move a key laterally while it was depressed, like a string player creating a vibrato. Film clips of Gould playing show him trying to do precisely that. Although the mechanics of the piano—any piano—make vibrato technically impossible to achieve, he was certain it could be done. To his delight, he decided there was more space between CD 174's keys than usual, thus enabling him to create a vibrato effect. The only explanation for this, Gould insisted, was that 174 must have been wider than the standard concert grand. Steinway's technicians refused to believe this could be the case. After all, in their dimensions Steinways were built to be as uniform as box cars. At Gould's suggestion, they measured the piano, only to discover it was indeed wider by three-eighths of an inch.

Gould made his landmark 1955 recording of the Goldberg Variations on CD 174 and subsequently had the piano sent around North America for many of his concerts. He increasingly despised everything about playing in public, especially in far-flung cities—the drafty halls, the unforgiving audiences, the unfamiliar accommodations, and the unpredictable quality of the pianos—so having CD 174 with him in such places was a comfort. If he couldn't control other circumstances of the concert life, at least, he thought, he could control the piano he played on.

When it proved impractical for Gould to take CD 174 with him to, say, St. Louis or Vancouver because of the cost of shipping, he would once again find himself at the mercy of the local Steinway dealer. In the early part of the twentieth century, the more heralded of the Steinway artists were able to travel with their own pianos on Steinway's nickel. In the 1950s, Henry Z. decided that Steinway should stop paying the thousands of dollars it cost to ship a piano around the country and to rely instead on the network of Steinway dealers. Like many other concert pianists, Gould came to judge a city not by its restaurants or art museums but by the quality of the Steinways one could find. And he was at his happiest as a concert performer when he was playing on his beloved CD 174.

But the honeymoon with CD 174 was cut tragically short when the piano was dropped at a freight depot en route back to New York from a concert in Cleveland and was damaged beyond repair. Gould mourned the loss of 174, and for months he was so out of sorts that the only consolation he found was in the old Chickering, which he continued to play at home.

Forced to resume his search for a concert grand that would suit him, Gould grew so frustrated that while recording Beethoven's C Minor Concerto he used three different pianos. Seasoned Steinway employees who thought they had seen it all were taken aback by Gould's unusual demands. Sascha Greiner complained in an internal memo that "Glenn Gould has been and is extremely difficult to satisfy with our instruments." Gould was so dissatisfied with every piano Steinway had to offer that one day in Toronto he went, pygmy chair in hand, to try out a few of the instruments at Heintzman, his hometown piano maker. Heintzman occupied a special place in the heart of many a Canadian musician, and when he arrived there, on short notice, Bill Heintzman himself escorted him to the artists' room, where he was treated like royalty. He played all the instruments Heintzman had to offer, but none felt right.

After CD 174, the piano that came closest to satisfying Gould was a Model D labeled CD 205, which he initially praised for having "a truly exotic range of tone, a magnificent melancholia, and, of course, great brilliance." But after a few months this piano, too, came to disappoint Gould, and he unleashed a torrent of criticism at Steinway. DC 205, he insisted, demonstrated a "wayward indifference" to his skill, an indifference Gould attributed to "a stiff action."

William Hupfer, Steinway's chief technician, once confessed to Gould that he had no idea what made an action loose or stiff. This prompted the pianist to write one of his most protracted—and unrealistic—pleas for help:

> *Frankly, I was appalled by the reluctance of your technical masterminds to make comparative judgments, to pronounce the relative success of one action over another. There are one or two pianos on which I have the illusion of complete premeditated controls and rapport. One is the old Chickering I*

have often told you about and which I am still using. Why couldn't some expert in physics make a comparative study of actions and alter the offending instrument accordingly? The problem is of some urgency to me. Now tell me, is there no one in all of Manhattan and its environs capable of analyzing what goes on in a piano action?

If last night was a success it was only because I conjured myself into a semi-trance by continuously murmuring— I'm playing the Chickering, I'm playing the Chickering, I'm playing the Chickering.

I now regard each keyboard I encounter with a faint chuckle, a connoisseur's relish of the wistful irony which has brought me to this stage and a deeper, dare I say more mature, understanding of the intriguing mixture of pedals, pins, and paradox which constitute the common piano.

Please, if you have compassion toward your fellow men and music makers, investigate this to the full.

I do hope that this letter has not been entirely dissolved in a guffaw. I am most anxious about it and will not rest easily till all is at right.

"Needless to say," he concluded, "you have my permission to reprint this letter in the Steinway monthly newsletter."

STEINWAY OFFICIALS POLITELY ignored Gould's suggestion that the company underwrite a scientific study of a piano's action, or even "discuss such a study with your supervisors of mechanical worries" (referring, of course, to Hupfer's department). Yet the company was accustomed to receiving complaints about its actions. In an 1892 tour, Ignacy Jan Paderewski, the Polish sensation, was nearly done in when he played 107 concerts in nearly as many days. He complained frequently about the stiff action of the Steinway that accompanied him on his tour, and referred to it as, simply, "my enemy." The piano nearly ended his career one night when he walked onto the stage, launched into the opening chords of his improvised prelude, and felt a searing pain shoot up his right arm. He finished the concert but played in constant pain, and before every concert thereafter he required electrical jolts. By the end of the tour he was playing with just four fingers of his right hand.

It was also the action that most bothered Gould about CD 205. "It requires a dispatch of considerable impetus to reach the bottom of the key in chord-playing, while such force requires, I feel, much greater resistance from the key to accommodate the pressure I must needs accord it. So unless I change my manner of playing (which would probably be healthier, cheaper and more comfortable) and become a typical triceps terror, I must conclude that 205 and I have attained the parting of the ways."

Gould traded CD 205 for another concert grand at Eaton's, CD 90. But the action on that piano was, in contrast to 205, much too loose. Again he put pen to paper, writing Steinway: "With my own flair for mechanical adjustment, I have made innumerable alterations which have been, of course, to the incalculable advantage of CD 90. These alterations have taken the form of deepening the key draft, in the hope of producing a reaction tantamount to a heavier touch. However, I am now totally unable and unwilling to play for even the briefest period on this instrument."

And once again the Chickering was invoked. After discontinuing his studies with his longtime teacher, Guerrero, Gould had moved the Chickering to his parents' lakeside cottage and entered into a full-blown infatuation with it.

"I need only mention parenthetically that my admiration, indeed my enraptured awe, at the interpretative versatility, the corrective faculty, the sheer exuberance of tonal palette offered by my subsidiary instrument, the worthy Chickering, remain undaunted," he wrote to his sponsors in New York. Steinway had heard way more than it cared to about the venerated Chickering. One executive suggested, in an internal memo, that Glenn Gould consult a psychiatrist who could, while the master was under hypnosis, repeat the word *Chickering* eighty-eight times.

For his part Gould felt not just spurned, but finally enraged, accusing Steinway of "incredible negligence . . . Surely no artist has ever received such lack of consideration, has so conspicuously failed to reap those advantages of personal consideration which, through popular legend, have become a trademark of Steinway & Sons."

Yet when Gould sensed he was complaining to the point of rankling, he tried to lighten up. "It is a sad commentary on the ungrateful turn of my ego that I should choose to combine a note of appreciation for your kindness with an epistle so full of complaint as to tax the perseverance of Job or any fine stoic martyrs you care to mention."

In early 1957, Steinway & Sons got a respite from the continual barrage of incoming mail from its most difficult artist when Gould took his first trip overseas for a two-week tour of the Soviet Union. He became the first North American musician to perform in post-Stalinist Russia, and his performances caused a major sensation. He gave his first concert at the Moscow Conservatory, playing a recital of Bach, Berg, and Beethoven. He was still unknown among Soviet audiences, and at the beginning of the concert the hall was only a third full. But once he sat down to play, starting out with four fugues from the *Art of Fugue* and the Partita no. 6, the audience grew increasingly excited. It was the first time many had heard Bach played in concert, and the audience was thunderstruck by the twenty-five-year-old pianist's originality, by the richness of dynamic nuance, and by the clarity of his playing. During the lengthy intermission, many people rushed out to call their friends, telling them to hurry to the concert hall. By the time the second half started, the hall was full. Gould finished to a thunderous, emotional ovation filled with rhythmic clapping and calls for encores. He played a Sweelinck fantasia and ten Goldberg variations before they allowed him to stop. Critics called his pianism "poetry" and "sorcery." For the rest of the tour, in Moscow and Leningrad, he played to sold-out audiences.

Gouldmania infected Russia, and for years afterward he was considered the greatest of the great among Bach interpreters. For Gould, not only was it rewarding to play for an audience that seemed to be holding its breath so it wouldn't miss any of the delicate shading in the music, but in Moscow he was pleasantly surprised to find the conservatory filled with an assortment of highly playable Steinways, many of them brought from Germany after the war. "Despite all language difficulties—cold halls, etc.—I really am having a wonderful time," he wrote in a postcard home to his parents. "Six encores in Leningrad despite a poor piano. The Steinway in Moscow was the most beautiful I have ever had."

From Russia, Gould continued on to Berlin, where he played Beethoven's C-Minor Concerto with the Berlin Philharmonic. Herbert von Karajan, the conductor, had been astonished by the Goldberg recording. Just as von Karajan had been besotted years earlier by the playing of Dinu Lipatti, the pianist whom the Columbia executive believed he saw reincarnated onstage when he attended Gould's Town Hall recital, he was entranced by Gould. After their first performance of the concerto, von Karajan pronounced it "masterly," but Gould disagreed. In contrast to what he experienced in Russia, Gould found the piano in Berlin less than ideal, and he claimed to be struggling against a sluggish action. But the German music critics did not seem to notice any such struggle and lavished praise on the performance. The critic for *Die Welt* went so far as to call it "one of those rare meetings with an absolute genius."

Word of Gould's overseas triumphs spread back to North America, and, of course, to executives at Steinway & Sons. As Gould's fame was rising meteorically it became even more important to placate the young pianist. Soon after his return home to Canada, Gould went to New York and was accompanied to Astoria by Henry Z. to try some of the new pianos. But after conceding that the tone was better on the newer models, Gould pronounced that not a single piano at the factory appealed to him. Henry Z., who was just getting to know the overly particular Mr. Gould, merely shrugged.

IN THE LATE 1950s, Gould instigated a small uprising among Steinway artists. At his urging, the Viennese pianist Paul Badura-Skoda, an established star, wrote to Steinway about the "dangerous extent" to which the number of poor pianos coming out of Astoria had increased. Badura-Skoda said that three out of every four of the Steinways he had recently played did not have enough resonance. And, he ominously added, "The black keys become narrower and narrower. If this trend continues, they will be like razor blades and pianists will cut their fingers to pieces." He also complained about the plastic keys that Steinway began using in the mid-1950s instead of ivory, which was growing scarce and was eventually outlawed. Some pianists, especially those who liked their keys just a little bit textured for better traction, reacted violently against the plastic, as it gave them nothing to hang on to. The plastic is "a most unhappy idea," Badura-Skoda complained. It "gets extremely slippery when wet. Together with the narrowness of the black keys, this causes literally thousands of wrong notes in performances."

Even worse, strings on Steinway pianos were breaking during concerts. It happened to Claudio Arrau, Rudolf Serkin, and Badura-Skoda. Steinway workers themselves acknowledged that the materials the company was getting did not equal the prewar quality. "We didn't have the influence with the manufacturers that we did before the war," Walter Drasche, a foreman in the action department, once told an interviewer. "Something was lost." Craftsmanship suffered as well, especially in the finish work.

In response to all these provocations, Gould did the unthinkable: He strayed. In St. Louis for a concert, Gould decided that none of the Steinways was adequate and called the Baldwin agency, whose representatives happily sent over two concert grands at no cost to Gould. Determined to underscore his discontent, Gould sent Steinway the bill for moving the Baldwin in and out of the St. Louis concert hall.

Steinway officials found the gesture unfathomably cheeky and refused to pay it. Sascha Greiner had been head of the Concert and Artists department for nearly three decades. And although he had a talent for remaining unflappable when working with temperamental pianists, this episode unhinged him. "This sort of thing must not be repeated," he wrote to Gould's agent. "An artist either plays a Steinway or he doesn't." And if a musician was to be called a Steinway artist, that meant that he played a Steinway at concerts, and no other instrument.

Gould was by no means the first Steinway artist with a wandering eye. In the 1870s, a pianist named S. B. Mills was contracted to Steinway but played two recitals in Pittsburgh on a Decker Bros. piano, and the local Steinway agent became irate when he got wind of it. In 1908, Paderewski, whom Steinway had brought to America from Poland for a lengthy tour in 1891 and pampered extensively, switched loyalties and moved, which infuriated top Steinway executives. And during a tour in the

1920s, when Arthur Rubinstein was unhappy with a Steinway in Chicago, he switched to a Mason & Hamlin. When Steinway found out, the company said he could not use its pianos for the rest of the tour. For several years, Steinway refused to let Artur Schnabel play its pianos in the United States unless he stopped playing Bechsteins in Europe.

When Gary Graffman was on tour, found the local Steinway unplayable, and didn't have CD 199 with him, he would sometimes use a Baldwin, to the consternation of David Rubin, who warned Graffman that he was jeopardizing his position with the Steinway company. "And the Steinway company is jeopardizing my livelihood," Graffman replied. Garrick Ohlsson went not once but twice to Bösendorfer. The second time, he was not invited back. "If you're affiliated you're affiliated, and that's the only structure we have," said Rubin. "If you're affiliated with another piano company, then don't play our piano."

Despite his occasional flirtations with other pianos— including a "top-secret" trip to the Bechstein dealership in Berlin, where he flirted with the idea of purchasing one of their pianos—Gould continued to search for the perfect Steinway. Other pianists, some professionals but many of them serious amateurs and fans, wrote to Gould suggesting he try out this piano or that, and Gould actually followed up on several of these tips in both Canada and the United States. His search took him to the Steinway Basement in New York more frequently than he preferred, and it was there that he fatefully tangled with Steinway's chief technician, William Hupfer.

Hupfer was a stocky, square-jawed, and boisterously friendly man who had already been working at Steinway for fifteen years when Glenn Gould was born. Eventually he worked his way up through the ranks of Steinway's tuning department, where he stayed for forty-nine years. Hupfer was a local kid, born and raised in Astoria. He came from a working-class family; both of his parents were immigrants from Germany. Hupfer played the piano as a young man, and in 1917, when he was offered a job in a Greenwich Village cabaret, his father panicked and taught him how to tune a piano instead. Soon after, he sent him to work for Steinway & Sons. Like Verne Edquist in Toronto, Hupfer started out as a chipper, doing the first rough tunings on the newly strung pianos on the factory floor. And like Edquist, he had a natural talent. One day, a foreman came over to check the young tuner's work. Deeply impressed after watching the speed and accuracy with which he brought the piano into tune, he commented, "Billy, I'll bet you could hear a flea sneeze." Hupfer's career was launched.

After Hupfer returned from the army during World War I, he went back to tuning in the factory. In 1925, perhaps sensing Hupfer's talent, a Steinway manager asked if he was interested in road work, which meant traveling with Steinway artists. He was taught how to regulate and voice as well as tune, and for four years he traveled with the great artist Myra Hess and two concert grands, shipping one ahead to the next city while the other was being used for a performance. In 1932, Hupfer took on a new job that was to last ten years: traveling with Rachmaninoff. Occasionally his job went beyond that of traveling tuner. During a cab ride to the concert hall in Montreal one night, Rachmaninoff turned to Hupfer and said, "You know, I have to play 'God Save the King' before I start playing the concert. Do you know how it goes?" Hupfer began humming it, and soon Rachmaninoff joined in. They kept it up for half an hour, until Rachmaninoff arrived at the concert hall. By 1946, Hupfer was elevated to the post of top concert man, not only because he had mastered his craft but because his temperament enabled him to get along with nearly everyone, even the most difficult concert pianists.

Henry Z. Steinway once observed that a good tuner had to

be part craftsman, part engineer, and part therapist. Steinway & Sons prided itself on developing tuners who understood that a pianist could get emotional, that after a long flight he could walk into a hotel room and, the afternoon before an important concert, sit down at the piano he's expected to play that night and lose his composure. As Steinway saw it, the technician couldn't simply say to the distressed artist, "Gee, I tuned it the best I can." A good technician says, "Gee, give me ten minutes." He might not actually make any improvements, but at least he can make the pianist feel better.

Hupfer was highly skilled at the human relations part of his job. It was rare for him to take a dislike to a pianist, and if he felt antipathy for Glenn Gould he kept it mostly to himself, grumbling only mildly to colleagues about what he considered to be Gould's unreasonable demands. In fact, he admired Gould because he was what Hupfer called a "presser," not a "hitter." Like Horowitz, Gould could get an amazing sound out of a piano with a very light touch. But Hupfer also believed that Gould ruined Steinway's pianos by demanding a touch so light that the instrument became unplayable for anyone but Gould himself. Hupfer had heard the dozens of stories about Gould running technicians around in circles, how he once even insisted that a technician replace the entire set of black keys because they "felt too narrow." Hupfer wasn't prepared to play along. "A Steinway is a Steinway," he said, "and that's what Glenn Gould is going to get." Gould, for his part, believed the company misunderstood the demands of his artistry. Years later, Henry Z., a man who always endeavored to see both sides of a debate, put it diplomatically: "Gould operated from himself out, and that could irritate a tuner."

Then came the shoulder incident.

Over the years, Gould's fear of germs and his obsession with his health had blossomed into full-blown hypochondria. David

Bar-Illan, the Israeli pianist, recalled once getting a phone call from Gould. Upon picking up the receiver, Bar-Illan first sneezed and then coughed before saying hello. With a note of worry in his voice, Gould asked, "What's the matter?" When Bar-Illan responded that he had a cold, Gould quickly hung up. Gould's hypochondriacal tendencies only increased with the years. He felt susceptible to drafts, which invariably led to a sore throat and chills. Symptoms, even if imagined, became real. He consulted many doctors throughout his life, but few brought relief. On many days he took his temperature every hour, and he believed it was better to live at the top of a hill because he would be less likely to develop cancer. He swallowed vitamins by the handful and always kept a dozen or so prescriptions as a preemptive measure against any and all health-related eventualities. Once, when his concert career was in full swing, he said he had left a concert hall too quickly, and as a result "caught such a cold in my face that I couldn't chew on the left side of my mouth for months."

Gould was particularly prone to musculoskeletal aches and pains, perhaps from a history of bad posture, and he took a multitude of prescription pills. He had often warned Steinway officials that he had an extreme sensitivity to physical contact, and his aversion to handshakes was well known throughout the organization. Anxious not to offend anyone by rejecting an outstretched hand, Gould finally resorted to a printed message that couldn't be misunderstood—or ignored. He had a little notice typed up and posted it to his dressing room door whenever he gave a concert. Occasionally he handed copies to fellow musicians and well-wishers after his performances. It read:

YOUR COOPERATION WILL BE APPRECIATED
 A pianist's hands are sometimes injured in ways which cannot be predicted. Needless to say, this could be quite serious.

Therefore—I will very much appreciate it if handshaking can be avoided. This will eliminate embarrassment all around. Rest assured that there is no intent to be discourteous—the aim is simply to prevent any possibility of injury.

Thank you.

GLENN GOULD

Gould had a particular phobia about Bill Hupfer, whose strong handshakes unnerved the young musician. It could have been that Gould was rattled by Hupfer's formidable physical presence, or that he sensed Hupfer's mild disapproval. Whatever the reason, Gould had gone so far as to let executives at Steinway know that Hupfer's handshakes made him especially anxious. One day in late 1959, while in New York, Gould dropped by the office of Winston Fitzgerald, an executive in the concert department with whom he was friendly. While Gould and Fitzgerald chatted, Hupfer came into the office to say hello. Hupfer knew by now to avoid a handshake. So, perhaps seeking a substitute that would still convey a warm greeting, Hupfer patted the pianist on the shoulder as he walked past him.

It could be that he underestimated the impact that any physical contact with Gould might have had, for the pianist immediately recoiled. "Don't do that," Gould said. "I don't like to be touched." Hupfer stood for an awkward moment or two, then stammered out an apology. Gould slumped in his chair and fell silent, but only briefly. After a minute or two, he had fully rebounded and carried on with the conversation. But later that day he called Fitzgerald to complain that Hupfer had hurt him when he placed his hand on Gould's shoulder. At first Fitzgerald, who was accustomed to Gould's persistent references to various physical ailments, thought little of it. But this was an "injury" that was not going away.

Gould started canceling concerts, including an entire European tour that was scheduled for February 1960. To spare Steinway the embarrassment, he told the press that he had dislocated his shoulder after a fall. But in his letters to Steinway, Gould blamed William Hupfer. Through his manager, Walter Homburger, Gould complained that the cancellations were "doubly unfortunate due to the fact that the injury was sustained in your hallowed offices and from the hands of one of your employees."

The following month Gould began traveling up and down the Eastern Seaboard, seeking treatment from a number of specialists, all of whom agreed that a nerve had been compressed by cervical vertebrae. None of the experts, however, was able to determine if the problem had come as a result of Hupfer's strong pat. In the spring of 1960, the still-ailing Gould went to Philadelphia to see a well-known orthopedic surgeon, who put him in an upper-body cast for a month, effectively immobilizing him. After the cast was removed he spent some time with his left arm in a sling and his neck in a cervical collar. Within a few weeks, despite continuing problems with his left shoulder, in June 1960 he resumed a heavy recording and performing schedule. He traveled to Detroit, Cincinnati, and Minneapolis, and recorded Beethoven's Tempest Sonata and Eroica Variations. The relatively quick rebound led to speculation among those who knew him that he might have been feigning his injury, or at the very least exaggerating its severity. But no one dared mention to Gould that some of the problem might be in his head, and for years afterward Gould's friends nodded politely when he complained of lingering shoulder problems that he traced to Bill Hupfer, whom he accused of nearly forcing him to give up playing the piano altogether.

For the rest of 1960, things returned to normal. Gould gave nearly two dozen performances that year and continued to search for a suitable concert grand for his recording sessions at

Columbia's studios on Thirtieth Street in New York. To no one's surprise, he wasn't particularly happy with any of the pianos he chose to try, but that seemed like business as usual. Then, just when all appeared to be forgotten, nearly a year after the encounter with Hupfer, Gould sued Steinway & Sons and William Hupfer for three hundred thousand dollars in damages. In the complaint, Gould's lawyers claimed that Hupfer had approached Gould from behind and "willfully or recklessly or negligently brought both his forearms down with considerable force on plaintiff's left shoulder and neck, driving plaintiff's left elbow against the arm of the chair in which he was sitting." As a result, the complaint continued, "plaintiff suffered serious injury to the nerve roots in his neck and spinal discs in the neck region . . . and was otherwise injured, was prevented from engaging in concert and recording performances, and suffered great pain of body and mind, which is continuing and may be permanent." The complaint stated that "on several occasions prior to December 8, 1959, plaintiff complained to defendant Steinway of the unduly strong handshakes and other demonstrative physical acts of defendant Hupfer toward plaintiff, and plaintiff demanded of Steinway that steps be taken to protect plaintiff from such dangerous acts of defendant Hupfer." But, the complaint stated, Steinway & Sons had done nothing.

Henry Z., who knew everyone involved, intervened quickly. The incident seemed to him at once bizarre and credible. Hupfer was a large man, to be sure, but Henry Z. doubted he had applied any real pressure at all, much less "considerable force," when he laid his hand on Gould's shoulder.

Henry Z. might have been worried, but he wasn't angry, in part because he was fond of Gould despite his eccentricities. He found him utterly likable—charming and completely devoid of malice—"no matter how nutty he is." He was also captivated by Gould's single-minded devotion to music. Though both Gould and Henry were fully tied to the Steinway company, the two could not have been more different. Henry would concede, with his trademark candor, that he could listen to a pianist play a Beethoven sonata and if he missed four notes, four lines, or four pages, he never would have known. But not because he wasn't listening. When Henry heard one of his pianos in concert, his attention was fixed on other things: Was the pedal squeaking? Was there a loose hinge on the lid? Were there other noises that shouldn't be there? Maybe he "couldn't tell whether Horowitz was any better than Gabrilowitsch," but he certainly appreciated Gould's musical genius.

The shoulder crisis, which presented a major public relations problem, sent the company into a lather. Gould was a much-loved pianist, but he was canceling so many concerts that he was annoying his fans. And he was showing up in newspaper photographs wearing a cast that ran from his abdomen to his neck. Reporters speculated that he might give up his concert career altogether.

When Henry Z. called Steinway's insurance company to notify them about the incident, he was shocked when the agent told him the injury would not be covered because it hadn't been reported in time. The company hadn't reported the incident, Henry Z. said years later, because, in spite of Gould's public pronouncements and conspicuous bandages, executives had merely chalked the entire episode up to the musician's hypersensitivity. "We had thought, Well, this is just Glenn Gould," recalled Steinway. "So we hadn't reported it." At this point, with no insurance coverage to back the company, "we were haggling absolutely alone. I was scared shitless." He took it upon himself to request a meeting with Gould, and late one summer afternoon in 1961, he and a Steinway lawyer went to a hotel in midtown Manhattan where Gould was staying. Gould had turned the air-conditioning off in his room and "it was hot as hell."

Making themselves as comfortable as possible, Henry Z. and the lawyer exchanged a few pleasantries with Gould, then the lawyer gently steered the subject to the matter at hand. Gould presented his demand. He was as affable as ever, perhaps even a little bit sheepish: He would drop the suit if Steinway agreed to pay his doctor bills and legal expenses. The total: $9,372.25. He did not ask the company to pay for lost concert income, which amounted to more than twenty thousand dollars. And he deducted one thousand dollars for the physiotherapist he had kept on call but never used.

Henry Z. had entered the meeting hoping to settle for half of Gould's initial claim, and as he sat there in his business suit in the stiflingly hot room, being asked to pay less than ten thousand dollars, something suddenly became clear to him: What mattered to Gould was that Steinway & Sons simply acknowledge that he had in fact been injured—and that they make him whole on the fees he had been forced to pay as a result of Hupfer's pat. It might have seemed like an inscrutable about-face, but given Gould's ongoing relationship with Steinway & Sons, whom he regarded much of the time as a paternalistic benefactor, it made sense. He was acting out of an almost childish yearning for recognition and fairness, and in doing so he bent over backward to be scrupulously fair himself. Still, it took Henry Z. by complete surprise. "When they came out with the amount I almost fainted," he recalled. "It was wonderful of him."

Hupfer was less conciliatory. Years later he remained bitter. "I never hit that man," he said in an interview. "I never hit anybody. Never. But I certainly would like to take a good punch at him now for being such a low-down rat."

After the episode was over with, Henry Z. wrote a summary of the incident, in which he observed, "In my opinion, this settlement is entirely due to Glenn's lack of any trace of a vindictive nature, and perhaps some feeling for Steinway & Sons at least trying to satisfy his piano needs."

Henry Z. didn't know it at the time, but Steinway was in fact very close to satisfying the great artist's needs. Just a few months before the shoulder incident was resolved, Gould had discovered a new Model D, made by the very company he had recently been battling and whose pianos he had so often reviled. He found it just a few miles from his home in Toronto, languishing in the corner of the backstage area of the Eaton Auditorium. But the piano was in disrepair. After years of being treated like an unwanted stepchild, it was now in need of a complete overhaul to get it back into concertworthy condition, and Gould had arranged to have it repaired at the factory in Astoria. Good relations with Steinway mattered more than ever, as Gould was determined to confirm arrangements with Eaton's and Steinway that he should use this piano exclusively. He had never been quite so smitten with a concert grand. Even the memory of CD 174 was eclipsed by the discovery of this remarkable new instrument. It went by the designation CD 318.

FIVE

Eaton's

By 1945, Eaton Auditorium had been open for more than a decade and critics deemed it one of the finest concert halls in Canada. Courtesy of Sears Canada.

How it was that CD 318 ended up in Toronto and not, say, Chicago, or the Steinway Basement, or someone's living room, is anyone's guess. Steinway's records do not reveal the reasoning behind a decision about where a piano is placed, only the fact of the decision itself. When the technicians were finally finished with the instrument—after it had been polished and fine-tuned for the final time and was ready to leave Astoria—it was March 1945, and not many people, after more than three years of war and its privations, were thinking about buying pianos, especially those costing thousands of dollars. (Steinway was selling its nine-foot concert grands for four thousand dollars at the time.) But new concert grands were always in demand among Steinway dealers, who strove to keep their piano banks filled with playable instruments. And in 1945, the Toronto Steinway dealership was in need of a new concert grand. So after its brief stint in the Steinway Basement, CD 318 was crated up and sent north to Canada via the American Railway Express Agency. A week or two later it arrived at the loading dock of the T. Eaton Company, Canada's premier department store, and joined the small but stately fleet of concert grands that resided on the store's third floor.

The rights to the exclusive Steinway dealership in Toronto had landed with Eaton's in the late 1930s. It was a privilege that had until then passed from one small piano dealer in the city to another. The arrangement with Eaton's, already a seasoned purveyor of pianos, seemed to Steinway & Sons the best one to date. Not only was Eaton's the largest and most popular Canadian department store, but its downtown Toronto location was the company's flagship. There were six floors of furnishings, clothing, and housewares and, to top it off—literally—a full concert hall on the seventh floor.

Eaton's was started by Timothy Eaton, a hardworking Irish immigrant who opened a haberdashery in Toronto in 1869, not long after Rowland Hussey Macy founded his first dry goods store in Haverhill, Massachusetts. A strict Methodist, Eaton allowed no tobacco or playing cards to be sold at Eaton's and, long after his death, the family kept the store closed on Sunday.

Eaton's eventually became a retail and social institution in Canada; by the 1930s, the company had opened stores across the country. It grew so huge, in fact, that at one point the store employed more people than did the Canadian government, and for several generations the members of the Eaton family were Canada's merchant royalty. Eaton's was well known for its customer service, as expressed in its long-standing slogan "Goods Satisfactory or Money Refunded." This included its pianos.

Throughout the 1930s and 1940s, it was not uncommon for large department stores to devote an entire floor to the sale of pianos: spinets, uprights, and baby grands. The family piano was as essential a purchase as the family car, sometimes more so, and in households across the economic spectrum the piano served as the hub of a family's social, artistic, and religious life and became a symbol of domestic refinement.

Even before the prestigious Steinway agency went to Eaton's in the 1930s, the retailer had been a major Canadian piano dealer. At one point in the early twentieth century, there were two dozen different piano manufacturers in Toronto alone, and Eaton's was an outlet for all of them. For a time, Eaton's even had its own house brand piano, an upright manufactured in Winnipeg. It was impossible to shop at Eaton's without being aware of the scores of pianos for sale.

Eaton's took its devotion to music a step further than most. The concert hall on the top floor of the Toronto store was the brainchild of Timothy Eaton's daughter-in-law, Flora McCrea Eaton, whom most employees referred to simply as Lady Eaton.

Built in 1930, the auditorium had 1,275 seats and quickly became renowned for its excellent acoustics.

The auditorium opened in 1931, and as early as 1932 Rachmaninoff came to play a concert of Scriabin, Haydn, and Beethoven. Canadian reviewers quickly deemed it one of the finest concert halls in Canada, and while it was smaller than Massey Hall, Toronto's main concert hall, Eaton Auditorium became a favored venue among performers. When Rudolf Serkin visited Toronto in 1937, he requested the Eaton venue over Massey Hall. Arthur Rubinstein did the same two years later. When Maria Callas sang at Eaton Auditorium, she charged what was at the time top dollar: six dollars a ticket. A particularly poignant recital was given by Artur Schnabel, a Jew who had fled Berlin in the 1930s. Schnabel came to Toronto on May 1, 1945, a week before Germany's unconditional surrender, and played Mozart, Beethoven, and Schubert. Glenn Gould, then twelve, so disapproved of Mozart that he decided not to attend the concert, and in so doing passed up his only chance to see his childhood hero play.

As was the accepted practice, whenever a pianist performed on a Steinway, Eaton's acknowledged the fact in its printed program and on the back cover featured a full-page ad for "The Instrument of the Immortals." Much as a sports manufacturer like Nike does today with top athletes, Steinway depended heavily on musicians to advertise its wares. Steinway artists may not have had "Steinway" stitched in gold on their coattails, but virtually all of the concert grands gave the brand ample exposure by featuring the company name in large gold lettering on the side of the piano that faced the audience.

Classical music wasn't the only cultural diversion that took place in the Eaton auditorium. There were travel lectures and plays, as well as the occasional offbeat production by entertainers like Carmen Amaya, a renowned "gypsy dancer" who had performed for President Roosevelt and took her act to Eaton's in the late 1950s. The Eaton Auditorium was also home to the annual Toronto Police Association show and the Sisters of the Good Shepherd Bingo Game.

Eaton's, like Steinway & Sons, had a talent for marketing. Borrowing the idea from William Steinway's clever layout of Steinway Hall in New York, which required concertgoers to pass through a showroom of pianos for sale while en route to the theater, the path to Eaton Auditorium took customers through the ladies' hats and men's suits departments before they arrived at the bank of elevators that ascended to the seventh-floor concert hall. When Lady Eaton had the auditorium renovated, adding plush velvet platform hangings, its acoustic vitality diminished drastically. Critics started complaining until finally, in 1968, the company brought in an acoustics consultant who recommended the installation of screens and drops that would better reflect the sound into the audience. But the cost—nine hundred dollars—seemed high, and the company chose not to have the work done.

The manager of Eaton's piano department was Clifford Gray, an ambitious man who put a great deal of energy into cultivating Eaton's relationship with Steinway & Sons. He regularly invited various members of the Steinway family up to Canada and entertained them at his farm outside Toronto. When Steinway & Sons celebrated its centennial in 1953, Gray talked Eaton's into putting on an elaborate concert in Toronto, with ten Steinway concert grands on the stage of Eaton Auditorium, arranged like a convocation of monoliths. He featured the "Immortals" slogan in Eaton's advertising, but he made sure to appeal to the more budget-minded customers as well by making clear that all of Eaton's pianos, especially the Steinways, could be bought on the installment plan.

The Steinway concert-bank program claimed to guarantee

Steinway artists a concert grand in any large city they traveled to, and most touring pianists remained dependent on the local supply of pianos to use in their performances. They also relied on the abilities of the local concert tuners. In Toronto, at Eaton's, this meant George Cook, a short, opinionated Scotsman who had arrived in Toronto in 1947 after learning that Canada was desperate for Steinway tuners after the war had ended. Cook had already spent two postwar years tuning his way through hundreds of Steinway grands, built by the Hamburg branch of the company, that had been neglected or abandoned during the war.

Already a highly proficient tuner when he arrived at Eaton's, Cook was instantly distressed by the quality of the concert pianos he was given to work with. Scores of European Steinways had been sent to New York after the war for reconditioning and resale, and Eaton's had taken half a dozen of them. The pianos were beautiful but problematic. After they had sat in cold, moist rooms in Europe and then traveled to the drier North American climate, the moisture evaporated from the pin blocks, which caused the tuning pins to come loose and the pianos to go out of tune only a few hours after a tuning. Like every other master technician, Cook had an ear for subtlety and appreciated that these massive, seemingly robust, even indestructible, instruments could be orchidlike in their fragility, prone to any assortment of ailments. He knew that anything could throw a great piano off, from the vagaries of climate to too little playing—or too much of the wrong kind of playing. And he understood that they required continual tending.

Cook believed that the situation was made worse by his employer's tendency to put profits before the upkeep of the instruments. He was appalled, if not particularly surprised, to discover that although the pianos belonged to Steinway, Eaton's brought in extra income by renting them out to far-flung concert halls all over Canada. All that shipping couldn't possibly be good for the instruments. With so many pianos in such frequent transit, it was all Cook could do to keep each one in acceptable condition. The more difficult task was keeping them finely tuned and ready for concert playing by the world's leading pianists. As a matter of fact, Cook was skeptical of the notion of a department store selling pianos in the first place, to say nothing of selling Steinways and maintaining an entire concert department.

Like other Steinway dealers, Eaton's tried to retire a concert grand before it got too old and worn, either sending it back to Steinway in New York in exchange for a new one or selling it from the showroom. By the time CD 318 arrived in Toronto from the Steinway basement in the mid-1940s, it joined Eaton's stable of three or four concert grands, all of them older than 318 and in various states of disrepair.

Cook arrived at Eaton's two years after 318 did. He was delighted with the piano, as well as another, CD 400. Both were exceptional, and both were easy to tune and to keep in tune, but Cook admired 318 in particular. Only a couple of years old when it arrived at Eaton's, it had not yet been played to death; its hammer felts were fresh, its sound vibrant, its action light. Cook knew that any pianist would be pleased with this piano; even those who preferred a heavier action came to admire 318 for its balanced tone and dynamic range.

ONE OF THE FIRST people Cook met in Toronto was Sir Ernest MacMillan, the Canadian musician and conductor who, upon hearing that Cook was the new concert tuner in town, asked, "Well, have you met our boy?" MacMillan was referring, of course, to the fifteen-year-old Glenn Gould, who was rapidly becoming a sensation. Cook had not met the "boy," nor had he heard of him. But that was soon to change.

One of Cook's first assignments from Eaton's was to go to Glenn Gould's house in Toronto to tune his Steinway B, a six-foot-eleven grand that had been built in 1934. It was "a crummy little thing," Cook later recalled. Nonetheless, he gave the piano a thorough tuning. While working, Cook noticed that one of the keys was sticking. He pulled out the action and retrieved a pencil that had lodged between the action frame and one of the keys. As he was preparing to slide the action back into the keybed, he looked up and saw a teenage boy standing quietly across the room, watching intently. Presumably this was the genius in question. The young pianist remained there and watched as Cook continued to work. Once Cook had finished tuning the piano to his satisfaction, the boy asked if the tuner would like to hear him play something. Without waiting for an answer, Gould seated himself on the bench and asked, "What would you like to hear, sir? The moderns?" Cook figured he meant jazz. But by "modern" the boy had meant Arnold Schoenberg, the Austrian composer who developed the composition technique of twelve-tone music, a system in which the pitch content of the music is determined by a particular arrangement of the twelve pitches of the chromatic scale without recourse to the harmonies of conventional key-centered tonality. The music mystified Cook. "He sat down at the piano and played and played and played," Cook recalled. "He had forgotten that I existed." For several years thereafter, as Eaton's concert tuner, Cook became, by default, Gould's unofficial tuner as well. But the one thing Cook didn't do—which Edquist of course would, some years later—was question the young pianist about his own preferences. What sort of features did he seek in a concert piano? And having failed to ask such questions, it never occurred to George Cook to match the youngster up with CD 318. In fact, the pianist and the tuner found they had little to say to each other.

And so the ideal pairing of CD 318 and Glenn Gould would be deferred for another decade.

ANOTHER MAINSTAY of Eaton's piano department was Muriel Mussen, who for thirty years was in charge of choosing the right instrument for visiting concert artists. A slight woman who remained unmarried throughout her life, Miss Mussen, as she was forever known, moonlighted as the organist with a local church. She drove to work in a little English Vauxhall each morning and hastened through the store—seldom lingering to glance at the merchandise—and up to the third-floor piano department. Mussen was often the first to learn that a famous pianist was coming to town, and if the performer didn't show up at Eaton's to pick out a piano, the task of choosing one fell to her. Though essentially a glorified secretary, as concert manager Muriel Mussen wielded considerable artistic power. She instinctively knew which piano to match with which artist. Of course, a pianist who wasn't likely to complain was easier to supply with an instrument than a prima donna who was spoiling for a fight, and she saw plenty of each. The highly demanding musicians usually got the best horse in the stable: CD 400, a piano that stayed in tune no matter how much of a pounding they gave it.

But her options were limited. She and her colleagues knew that Steinway had a habit of sending its outlying distributors the lesser instruments, the ones that never quite managed to please a critical mass of pianists no matter how much Steinway tinkered with them in New York. Those less-favored pianos got sent out to Cincinnati or down to Atlanta. Or up to Toronto.

On occasion she suffered a lapse in judgment. When Carmen Cavallaro came to town, Mussen, who was unfamiliar with his extensive classical training, dismissed him as a flashy pianist of

popular songs and sent CD 226 up to the auditorium. It was a particularly bad specimen that refused to stay in tune; often within
minutes of a tuning, its temperament had queered. And it wasn't
many minutes into Cavallaro's concert before he began to notice.
When perfectly in tune, the three strings composing a single note
seem as if they are one, all sounding exactly the same pitch in a
clean, clear unison. But before Cavallaro had even finished his first
piece on the program, after some moderate pounding, the strings
had slipped slightly and the notes started to wobble. What was
perceived at first as one pure note now started to sound shim-
mery and metallic, and then, as it worsened, developed into a
rolling dissonance. Audiences seldom notice when a piano goes
out of tune. But many concert pianists with well-trained ears do.
In the case of CD 226, the condition could perhaps be traced to a
poor stringing job done at the factory. Whatever the cause, not
only did Cavallaro notice the problem, he threw a fit after the concert, sending word to Clifford Gray, who forwarded the complaint
to Mussen, who in turn made a note to herself to suggest to Cavallaro that, should he come to Toronto again, he might like to
stop by Eaton's to choose a piano himself.

No ONE KNOWS for sure when Glenn Gould first played CD 318.
It's possible that in 1946, when the thirteen-year-old Gould, still
young and eager, took the stage in Massey Hall to play at a
Toronto Conservatory concert, it was CD 318 that Muriel
Mussen sent across town. At the time the instrument itself was
also young: The pedals were snug in their bearings, the new
parts were all in alignment, and the piano had a clear, strong
tone. Or CD 318 could have been the instrument Gould was
given the following year when he made his January 1947 debut
with the Toronto Symphony Orchestra in the same hall. Whatever the piano, he caused a sensation. Conjuring the great Russian

Vladimir de Pachmann, who had a remarkable ability to alight on the keys without a hint of strain, one reviewer wrote of Gould: "Last evening his butterfly hands made the piano sing as only de Pachmann used to do." Or it could have been later that year that Mussen sent CD 318 upstairs for Gould's first professional recital in the Eaton Auditorium, for which people paid three dollars for the best seats in the house to hear the talented boy play Scarlatti, Beethoven, and Chopin. Then again, she might have given him the dreaded CD 226.

At Eaton's, CD 318 enjoyed many years as a favored child. It was no magical instrument like CD 400, but pianists seemed to like, and even request, it for concerts. But gradually it too began to suffer the effects of age and overuse, having been sent all over Canada to endure countless hot and humid summers followed by dry, chilly winters. Over more than a decade of punishing use, the piano developed battle fatigue. The hammers became so grooved and worn, and the strings so distressed, that the instrument began producing abysmal zinging and dull tones.

And pianists—especially the fortissimists who had little appreciation for 318's delicate action—began to notice. George Cook recalled how, in the middle of the 1950s, Myra Hess came to town to play at Massey Hall and, after sitting down to play 318, immediately recoiled in disgust. "This is a terrible piano, my boy, can't you do anything about it?" she asked him. "I'm just the piano tuner," he replied, and, unable to resist a jab at Eaton's, he added, "And don't forget you're dealing with a department store."

In the late 1950s, Clifford Gray traveled to New York to meet with Fritz Steinway, who was then in charge of the Concert and Artists department, to discuss the many complaints he was receiving from musicians who came through Toronto. Some of the pianos—and CD 318 in particular, Gray pointed out—had been at Eaton's for more than a decade. Steinway agreed they should all be

exchanged for new pianos. Gray's complaint was perfectly in keeping with the Steinway & Sons philosophy that a concert grand was
generally considered to have outlived its usefulness in the concert
hall after six or seven years. The company knew that a concert pianist wanted an instrument that was at its peak performance, suitably seasoned but not over the hill. Ten years was the very outside
extreme of a concert grand's performance life. And here was CD
318, going on fifteen years in more or less continual use.

But Steinway was still recovering from the effects of a protracted strike by its factory workers, and the work-flow cycle
meant that an exchange would have to wait until the next concert season. Fritz Steinway assured Gray that Eaton's would get
the next new piano that rolled off the factory floor.

For the previous several years, Eaton's retail piano department had been shrinking as the store made more room for
boats, televisions, and record players on its display floors. Gray
was so disconcerted by this trend that he went to New York
again, this time to visit his U.S. counterparts at Macy's and Gim-
bel's. They too complained that they were seeing their piano inventory lose ground to the latest in color televisions, radios, hi-fi
systems, and records. Both stores reported that piano sales had
dropped to a level that they hadn't seen since the Depression.
Gray knew how serious, and irreversible, the trend had become
when, in 1956, the cellist Mstislav Rostropovich came to town
and the back cover of the concert program, which always featured an advertisement for "The Instrument of the Immortals,"
now promoted Stromberg-Carlson High Fidelity Radios,
Phonographs, and Televisions.

But the diminishing demand for pianos in people's homes did
not reduce the need for playable concert grands. By the late
1950s, after endless complaints from George Cook and nearly fifteen years into its life in Toronto, 318 had fallen into sufficient
disrepair that Clifford Gray finally instructed Muriel Mussen to

write to Steinway and get the thing sent back once and for all. The piano was taken out of circulation entirely and banished to a backstage recess in Eaton Auditorium. There it sat with its lid down, awaiting its return to New York, where it would be refurbished, stripped of its CD status, and sold as a used Model D.

FROM THE MOMENT when Glenn Gould first began touring in earnest, in the mid-1950s, he began to have thoughts that he would have to give up performing because there were no pianos he could bear to play. But rather than abandon his career, he developed a means of compensating for this problem away from the keyboard.

Gould was unique among pianists in that he never felt a compelling need for constant access to a piano. He had an extraordinary ability, developed long ago as a young student with his teacher Alberto Guerrero, to study a score and automatically associate it with a specific tactile response. He could read a piece of sheet music, then go straight to the piano and play it perfectly with limber, knowing hands. "When I haven't played for a few weeks the nicest moments I have are when I first sit down to play," he once told an interviewer. "I have never understood the stiff-finger syndrome or whatever it is people talk about, because during all of however many weeks that may have elapsed without playing, there is no hour of the day in which some music doesn't enter my head and instantly get translated into a kind of spontaneous finger system."

Still, he knew what he was looking for in a piano. Gould didn't necessarily want an instrument with a big sound, even when he was playing in large halls. He preferred pianos whose sound might be described as "puritan": not dry, exactly, or constrained, but clear and detached. But Steinway concert grands typically sounded just the opposite, with a growling, powerful bass and a brilliant treble.

Gould developed his ability to "play" away from the instrument because he was convinced that every piano other than his beloved Chickering had an inadequate action. Knowing this distracted him enough that he couldn't play well. Or so he believed. Powerless to change this unfortunate circumstance, he resorted to unusual tricks of the imagination.

Such was the case in Israel in 1958, when Gould went to Tel Aviv to play a series of recitals and orchestral appearances with the Israel Philharmonic. The schedule—nine concerts in eleven days—was grueling enough. But the piano he was given to play was, he later recalled, possibly the worst concert instrument he had ever encountered. After the third performance, Gould got to the point where he felt like he could no longer control it.

"It was running away from me," he told an interviewer years later. "It was like a car with power steering and I was a driver who was used to a stick shift. And it was frightening."

Gould determined to reinstate his mental image of some other instrument while continuing to play the concerts on the dreadful piano in Tel Aviv. And of course the piano of his dreams was the Chickering.

So he drove up to Herzliya, a city on the Mediterranean fifteen miles north of Tel Aviv, and found a sand dune facing the sea. There he sat in a Hertz rental car, trying to feel and recall the precise sight, sound, and tactility of his Chickering at home. In his mind, without moving one finger, he played through the entire Beethoven B-flat Major Concerto, which he was to play that night on the brutish piano in Tel Aviv. While he sat there, he later reported, he felt himself to have really been playing the music.

That evening he went to the concert hall, sat down, and began to play. For the first few phrases, he was horrified to discover that the keys were barely being depressed, because he was moving his fingers in relation to his memory of the Chickering's touch and not the piano he happened to be seated at. But once he adjusted to the instrument at hand, "something came out that was really quite extraordinary."

After that evening's concert, he was visited backstage by Max Brod, who had been the close friend and literary executor of Franz Kafka, a writer Gould greatly admired. Brod's companion, a woman named Ester Hoffe, told Gould in a thick German accent that she and Brod had been to his other performances, and this time he had seemed different, somehow removed. He thanked her, smiled, and bowed deeply.

In Tel Aviv, perhaps, Gould was resigning himself to what seemed to be emerging as a central fact of his concert-playing life: No piano would be ideal, and he might have to rely on mental tricks such as the one he resorted to on the Herzliya sand dune. But as it turned out, he would never again need to conjure the Chickering's feel.

No one could attest to having been at Eaton's with Glenn Gould two years later, in June 1960, when he discovered CD 318. It could well have been that, weary of Gould's unhappiness with everything the New York pianos had to offer, Clifford Gray—or perhaps Muriel Mussen—urged him one afternoon to go upstairs to the auditorium to have a look at old 318, which was still there, waiting for its trip back to Steinway & Sons. Or maybe he had some other reason to be in the auditorium, spotted the piano backstage, wandered up to it, lifted the fallboard, sat down, and started playing. However it was that he encountered the piano, once he began playing, his memory was jogged. He *recognized* this piano. He knew he had played on it before, many years earlier. His ears now remembered its refined sound: the lovely, singing treble and clean, taut bass. And his fingers recalled its extreme responsiveness. For all those years, he had scoured New York, not Toronto, for the perfect piano. And here it was. Yes, it needed work, but it was the kind of work that could easily be done in a few weeks in New York. Gould immediately decided to make his next recording on CD 318, and he made plans to ship the piano to Steinway for its rehabilitation.

On June 22, 1960, Gould wrote a letter to Winston Fitzgerald in the Concert and Artists division at Steinway. Instead of offering his usual complaints, he regaled Fitzgerald with his rapture upon rediscovering his old acquaintance CD 318. He couldn't resist injecting some tongue-in-cheek self-aggrandizement as well:

> *Dear Professor Fitzgerald:*
>
> *This is just a note to remind you that before you leave on Part I of your vacation, before in other words the efficiency of Freres Steinway plummets noticeably, I would be grateful if you would make sure that all is in readiness for the arrival of CD 318.*
>
> *I don't have to enumerate for you the many admirable qualities of this klavier, suffice it to say it was the piano which assisted in many of the memorable moments in my career as child prodigy. For this reason alone I expect it to be given a place of honour in the basement and that Morris Schnapper will be required to bow twice each time he passes it. For the exhibit in your showroom, I could if you wish send a picture of myself in the Lord Fauntleroy suit—the sort of garb with which I was usually decked out by my doting parents for performances on 318.*

The search for just the right piano had ended in thrilling success, and years of perpetual refinement were about to begin.

SIX

A Romance
on Three Legs

Master piano technician Rhys McKay voicing a
newly restored 1904 Steinway Model O at
Callahan Piano in Oakland, California, in 2007.
Courtesy of www.callahanpiano.com.

This piano has a very light action, as indeed all pianos that I prefer do. Many people say it's tinny and sounds like a harpsichord or a fake harpsichord or God knows what. Maybe it does. I think it has the most translucent sound of any piano I ever played.

—Glenn Gould

IT WAS ON AN AFTERNOON IN 1962 that Glenn Gould entered Verne Edquist's life.

When Edquist started the job at Eaton's a year earlier, he had been told that Gould would be among the many musicians in town whose pianos he would be looking after. And one afternoon, Muriel Mussen sent Edquist to Gould's apartment to tune the Chickering. As Toronto's hometown hero, Gould was accorded many favors. The tuners at Eaton's had grown all too familiar with the finicky, eccentric pianist and with the pianos in his life, including the Chickering. Although that piano was not, strictly speaking, the responsibility of Eaton's, when Glenn Gould asked for an Eaton's tuner, someone was always immediately dispatched. It didn't matter what piano they were being asked to work on; with Gould, the answer was always yes.

Of course, Edquist knew of Gould. Everyone in Toronto did. Mostly he knew about the pianist's notoriety as an "unusual individual," as Edquist put it years later. He vividly remembered the time, so many years before, when the young Gould had come to Heintzman in search of a concert grand that he could comfortably perform on. But Edquist had no special knowledge of Gould's playing, and certainly no special insight into what made him an artistic genius. He wasn't particularly interested in whatever it was that distinguished Gould's playing from anyone else's, and he wasn't intimidated by Gould's reputation. "At that point in my career, one piano player was pretty much the same as any other," he said. "I hadn't yet learned to interpret their nuances." So, although he knew that he was going to tune the piano of Canada's most famous living musician, he was, if not blasé, at least relaxed. Armed with nothing more than a bag of tools and his growing self-confidence as a piano tuner, Edquist set off to tune the fabled Chickering.

Gould may have loved and revered the Chickering, but he neglected it. He refused to have any work done unless it was falling apart. Edquist knew that he wasn't the first to try to work on the old instrument: Many others had come before him, but the piano refused to hold a tuning. When Edquist arrived at Gould's penthouse, he found that the middle registers were passable, but the rest of the piano was dramatically out of tune—even more than he had expected. When he heard about the journey it had made, he wasn't surprised. Gould had recently had the piano moved to Toronto from his family's drafty cottage at Lake Simcoe, a ninety-minute drive north from Toronto. In the overheated apartment, the wood had shrunk. This, in turn, had loosened the tuning pins so much that they wouldn't stay in place for more than a few hours before slipping in the wooden pin block.

Other technicians had tried to solve—or, more accurately, mask—the problem by muting the strings that wouldn't stay in tune. Edquist tried that too, at first. But as he worked his way through the piano, he found that many more strings would have to be muted, which in turn would have altered the fundamental sound of the instrument. Edquist decided the piano should be sent to the Eaton's repair shop, where larger tuning pins that wouldn't slip could be installed. He presented his proposed remedy to Gould.

But the pianist would have none of it. All Gould wanted, he told the tuner, was that Edquist do what had been done hundreds of times before: get the instrument into playable condition, even if it was only for the time being. Further, Gould explained, it was only the middle octaves that were of real importance: He played mostly Bach on the Chickering, and since Bach had composed on a keyboard that was about three octaves narrower than the modern piano, the middle of the keyboard was all that Gould needed in good condition. But Edquist, a perfectionist himself, had no interest in compromise. Experience told him what the piano needed and he was not going to settle for a half measure when he knew what the right course of action was. Nor was he going to stand there and argue with the most famous classical musician Canada had ever produced.

"Are you telling me you are refusing to tune the piano?" Gould asked, taken aback.

"Yes," Edquist replied matter-of-factly.

When recalling the encounter years later, Edquist confessed that he had acted like "a bull in a china shop." But he was adamant about doing the job correctly and was unwilling to pander to a celebrity. Still, he sensed that in his blunt wake he had left behind an extremely unhappy customer.

Gould called for a taxi and Edquist returned to Eaton's. Certain he was going to be fired, he decided to take a preemptive approach. He went directly to Clifford Gray and told him that if his job depended on saying yes to Glenn Gould, no matter the circumstance, he would like to know now so that he could rethink his employment situation. Rather than fire him, Gray was amused. He knew he had a talented, uncompromising tuner on his hands, and he had heard enough from other tuners about the derelict condition of Gould's Chickering to agree that Edquist had done the right thing.

In fact, rather than irk Gould, Edquist had made a significant impression on him. After that, when requesting a tuner from Eaton's, whether for the Chickering or his other personal piano, the seven-foot Steinway Model B that George Cook had previously attended to, Gould insisted that they send Edquist and Edquist only. Edquist's relentless insistence on doing things his way—which, as it almost always turned out, was the right way—set him apart from other tuners. Some, like George Cook, may have shared a stubborn streak, but none were inclined or able to push back on a top artist and invoke their own technical expertise when the moment required it. The encounter over the Chickering galvanized what was to become a decades-long association between the willful artist and the dedicated technician.

Months after that first trip to Gould's apartment, Edquist was vindicated when the Chickering showed up at the repair shop at Eaton's and the tuning pins were replaced, as per Edquist's original prescription. Edquist never asked Gould what prompted him to send the piano in, but he enjoyed his small triumph for years afterward.

The first time Edquist encountered CD 318 was not long after the tussle over the Chickering. Gould was preparing for a CBC recording and he wanted 318 tuned and regulated right away. When Edquist expressed surprise that he hadn't seen or worked on this instrument before, Gould reminded him that it had been exiled to the corner of Eaton Auditorium before Edquist arrived at Eaton's.

Gould was anxious to hear the tuner's appraisal of the piano. And he was delighted to discover that Edquist was as impressed by it as he was. Edquist, of course, had the advantage of not being distracted by the sight of the piano's battle scars, its scratches, dings, and other evidence of years spent on the road, hard at work. Edquist couldn't understand what George Cook had been complaining about. It was true that the hammers hadn't been replaced for many years, but what he instantly recognized in this instrument was its near-perfect embodiment of the ideal Steinway tone.

Striking a key on the piano, however, Edquist, like Gould, knew that there was something about CD 318 that set it apart even from other Steinways. Usually Edquist set his ear for nuances in pitch, resonance, and overall quality of tone. It was a dispassionate approach, but efficient. While Edquist encountered fine Steinways every week, the first few chords he played on 318 got his attention. He was well accustomed to the different qualities of fine instruments, but in 318 the tone and the featherlight, fast-repeating action stood out. This was a piano with a soul.

It had been nearly two years since the piano had gone to New York for a thorough going-over, and now Edquist settled in for a full tuning and regulation. First he gave the piano a quick rough tuning; then he lifted off the key slip, the long, narrow wooden strip in front of the keys. Next he removed the two screws from beneath the treble and bass cheek blocks, the two rectangular blocks at either end of the keyboard. This enabled him to lift the fallboard from the piano, exposing the action mechanism inside. Then he slid the entire sixty-pound action out and onto his lap.

Wearing strong magnifiers pressed against his glasses, he took a small sandpaper file and reshaped each of the eighty-eight hammers, which had been lined with grooves after more than fifteen years of hitting the strings. Then he adjusted and aligned hundreds of individual action parts. In order to approach those parts from a series of different angles, he moved the action from place to place—onto his lap, then onto a workbench, then back onto his lap. And to test the action as he went, he often slid it back into the piano, then removed it again to make more refinements, including voicing and fitting hammers to individual strings so that all three strings of each note would be set in motion at precisely the same time. Once he was satisfied with the hammer-to-string fit, he isolated notes that sounded overly bright and needled the corresponding hammers. For notes that sounded dull, he filed the wool, ironed it quickly with a clothes iron, or even added a little lacquer to it until he was satisfied that the tone was even and consistent from bass to treble.

Once he had replaced the action for the last time, he gave the instrument a fine-tuning. The process took several hours, and the improvement was dramatic. When Edquist sat and played major and minor chords, first delicately, then forcefully, up and down the keyboard, he was still more impressed by CD 318's sound. The piano was producing an extraordinary clarity of tone.

Somehow the soundboard, built to perfection from Alaskan Sitka spruce, did more than perform its basic function of amplifying the sound of the strings: Strong and flexible, it produced sounds that were not only rich but soulful. The piano had a glorious, full-bodied singing treble and a magnificent, refined bass. Still more impressive were the piano's harmonics—the higher-pitched overtones, sometimes more pronounced than the fundamental tone, that are heard when a single note is played and which are among the key determinants of a piano's character and sound. CD 318 had some of the most beautiful overtones Edquist had ever heard. Still more impressive, when the piano was fine-tuned, the harmonic balance between bass and treble was absolute. The piano was literally bursting with vibrant colors. Although this nine-foot, twelve-hundred-pound, beaten and weary behemoth stood stock-still, Edquist knew the instrument was very much alive. Gould, in turn, was captivated by what he described as its "translucent sound," the "clarity of every register," and the incisiveness of its articulation. He had once said he was happiest when the sound of a piano appeared to be "a little like an emasculated harpsichord." And 318 achieved that sound like no other piano he had ever found, making it beautifully suited to music, such as the compositions of Bach, that had been written for harpsichord.

CD 318's refinement of tone also enabled Gould's genius for playing contrapuntal music, with its independent voices—a signature feature of the Bach repertoire. The piano didn't have the throbbing, singing tone and earth-shattering bass that pianists prized in so many Steinways.

But most of all Gould loved the piano's featherlight action, which had been carefully constructed back in Astoria in 1943. One of the most important variables in a piano's action is the amount of resistance it enables a pianist to feel beneath his fingers. Arthur Rubinstein, for instance, never picked an easy, light action when he was selecting a Steinway. He always chose an unwieldy piano that required him to work it like a beast and apply considerable downward thrust to get the round, sostenuto, cantabile sound he wanted. As David Rubin once observed, Rubinstein always created his best sound when his arms were working their hardest. But Gould, never a pounder, wanted to expend a minimum of energy while playing. As Edquist became fond of saying, Glenn Gould would have been happy if the piano would just play itself for him.

CD 318's extra-light action made it especially well suited to early music: It permitted Gould to articulate with subtlety and precision, which is essential when creating contrapuntal textures. When he pushed a key down, he got a remarkably clean sound, and when he let the key off, 318's extraordinarily effective damping mechanism stopped the sound instantly—it didn't bleed over the way many pianos do, creating a permanent halo of tone. And that was exactly how Gould liked it. He wanted the piano to produce sound when he told it to and to cease the instant he signaled it to stop. He wanted absolute control over every nuance of tone and phrasing, and an instant and attentive response to whatever his fingers dictated. In that respect, 318's action was ideal.

Like Gould, Vladimir Horowitz preferred a shallow, highly responsive action that sent the keys down at the slightest touch.

Horowitz's reputation as a technical genius rested largely on the lightning speed of his omniscient fingers, combined with a precision that reflected an uncanny rhythmic acuity. The only way to achieve this effect was on a piano that could respond to the lightest possible touch.

Despite their shared preference for light piano actions, however, Gould and Horowitz were miles apart when it came to musical taste. Gould was usually generous in his praise of the many fellow artists whose preferences differed from his own, but he was consistently scornful of Horowitz, who represented everything Gould considered wrong with the standard piano repertoire. Of Horowitz's famed octave technique, in which he played scales in octaves at blinding speed, Gould once grumbled, "He fakes them." It is true that there are little tricks that pianists, including Horowitz, have been known to indulge in to get a certain effect. For example, when playing scales that quickly sweep up the keyboard, the musician can increase the overall speed by strategically dropping an occasional note in order to eliminate the classic fingering that would necessitate slowing down. It's doubtful that Horowitz seriously faked much of anything in his playing, but Gould couldn't resist a catty swipe at his archrival, and in the 1970s he went so far as to present his sponsors at Columbia Records with the idea that he record a parody of Horowitz's triumphant return to the concert stage after a hiatus of several years. Columbia soundly rejected the notion, sniffing that to do so would be "undignified."

Horowitz returned Gould's disdain. Upon hearing the younger pianist's 1973 recording of Wagner's *Siegfried Idyll*, which some consider to be one of Gould's greatest performances, Horowitz told the *New York Times*'s Harold Schonberg, "He played like a stupid ass."

Ironically, it may well have been Vladimir Horowitz whom Gould had to thank for CD 318's extreme responsiveness. As

Henry Z. Steinway would recount, it was when Horowitz first showed up on the U.S concert scene in the late 1920s, and personally demanded a springier keyboard, that Steinway departed from its norm and began producing accelerated actions.

CD 318's extreme evenness inspired Gould to record works he might otherwise have avoided. Among the pieces that Gould first taped on CD 318 were ten Brahms intermezzi—complex, lavishly romantic pieces, some of which Brahms had called "lullabies to my sorrows." The intermezzi were standard fare for many pianists. While Gould performed and recorded quite a bit of Brahms, he disliked many of the composer's works, such as the flashy variation sets and the big early sonatas. But he admired the gentleness and restraint of the intermezzi. His interpretation of them was peculiarly intimate and stood in stark contrast to his more austere side, which he most famously exhibited when playing Bach. He told an interviewer that he played the intermezzi "as though I were really playing for myself, but left the door open." He played them with all the nostalgia and melancholy that Brahms had intended—with great rhythmic power as well as close attention to tone and color. Gould himself was extremely proud of the record, pronouncing it "the sexiest interpretation of Brahms intermezzi you have ever heard." Indeed, it became one of his most popular albums ever.

Brahms was also the composer who prompted the biggest cause célèbre in Gould's concert career. In early 1962 he was scheduled to play Brahms's monumental Concerto in D Minor with the New York Philharmonic. Of course he would use CD 318. In advance of the performance, Gould called the conductor, Leonard Bernstein, to let him know that his interpretation would be more contemplative than most, with far slower tempi than usual. Bernstein's ideas about the piece were more conventional than Gould's, but he was willing to play it Gould's way and alerted his orchestra accordingly. Seeking to explain Gould's interpretation, Bernstein did something highly unorthodox: Before the performance, he gave a four-minute speech to let the audience know that his ideas and Gould's had collided over the piece—but "because Mr. Gould is so valid and serious an artist . . . I must take seriously anything he conceives in good faith," he said, adding, "I have only once before, in my life, had to submit to a soloist's wholly new and incompatible concept, and that was the last time I accompanied Mr. Gould." Gould then walked onstage as the audience cheered. But the critics were brutal, condemning Gould's performance as "funereal." "The Gould boy played the Brahms . . . slower than the way we used to practice it," Harold Schonberg wrote in the *Times*. But Bernstein, who adored Gould, defended his musician. "I never loved him more," he later wrote.

The incident didn't help endear Gould to concert life. Despite critical acclaim and amazing popular success, as an adult Gould experienced agonizing discomfort over performing in public. In the early 1960s his concert schedule got lighter and lighter, although he always considered it too heavy. In 1961, he gave twenty-six performances in seventeen different cities and found it increasingly enervating. He had an especially terrible time with unfamiliar beds. A mattress with a "bad action" could cause him to call the front desk for a new one at four A.M. He also hated to fly, and in 1962 he swore off airplanes altogether. If he had to travel far, he took a train.

Of course, in hating the touring life he was far from atypical. No performer believed that he played his best in an unfamiliar concert hall, on a bad piano, at the end of a grueling cross-country tour, after a bad night on a spongy hotel bed and an unsatisfying rehearsal with an incompetent conductor. What set Gould apart was how vocal he was on the matter. His teacher Alberto Guerrero had discouraged his students from pursuing concert careers. Gould had come to hate the risk taking associated with live performances and grew tired of what he called the "non-take-two-ness" of the concert experience. He believed that people were just waiting for him to mess up, and he resented it. "To me this is heartless and ruthless and senseless. It is exactly what prompts savages like Latin Americans to go to bullfights," he once said. Gould also said that large concert halls were exactly the wrong place for the complex, intimate music he liked to play.

At the same time that he lightened his concert load, he found that he enjoyed recording more and more. Unlike a concert stage, Gould found the recording studio to be a collaborative place, with pianist, sound engineers, technician, and producers all working together to create something close to perfection. Very quickly he settled into his element as a recording artist, recording, in 1962 and 1963, Bach's partitas and book one of the *Well-Tempered Clavier* as well as concertos by Schoenberg and Mozart. But Gould didn't merely record LPs. He became a zealous advocate for the promise of recording not just as a means to augment live performances but as something that could—and should—supplant them altogether.

For years he talked about quitting the concert-tour circuit. His cancellations grew more frequent, his excuses more outlandish. In 1961 he withdrew from a scheduled appearance with the Philadelphia Orchestra, explaining that he had developed a serious phobia about playing in that city. Some people close to Gould speculated that this was because Philadelphia was where he had seen the specialist who had put him in the large cast after the incident with Bill Hupfer.

Perhaps Gould was aware of the fate met by the brilliant pianist Josef Hofmann, who by 1946 had played a concert so hamhandedly that people demanded their money back. (Afterward, undeterred, Hofmann sent Steinway a telegram pronouncing the concert the greatest triumph of his career.)

Or it could have been that Gould was haunted by what had happened in 1939 to Paderewski's "million-dollar hands," when, at age seventy-nine, the nearly destitute virtuoso had embarked on an American concert tour out of sheer financial desperation. Thirty years earlier he had had the concertgoing public at his feet. "Paddymania" had inspired ad campaigns for shampoo and candy, even a miniature windup toy of the pianist himself. But now as he sat onstage, haggard, with bent head and vacant stare, Paderewski played with what Sascha Greiner of Steinway later described as "a pathetic dreariness." Two years later Paderewski was dead, and his Steinway went on display at the Smithsonian.

More likely, though, Gould simply grew to dread performing in public so intensely that the possibility of leaving it all behind and never looking back was a huge relief. And why not? After all, Franz Liszt, the first real modern concert artist of the piano, quit the concert tour at age thirty-six, calling it a "traveling circus life." And Gould felt much the same. Someone once remarked that Gould preferred talking nonsense about anything at all, anywhere at all, to playing the piano marvelously in the concert hall. Many speculated that if Gould hadn't been so determinedly reclusive, and had he not so detested giving concerts, his popularity would have been all the greater. But popularity did not mitigate his growing fears about performing, and into the early 1960s he was not only reducing bookings but increasing cancellations as well.

In 1963, he gave just nine concerts in five cities. In March of 1964, he played in Chicago. Two weeks later, on April 10, he gave a recital at the Wilshire Ebell Theater in Los Angeles. Edquist didn't accompany him on that trip, but CD 318 did. For that concert, to a near-capacity audience, he played a typical program: four fugues from the *Art of Fugue,* Bach's Partita no. 4 in D Major, Beethoven's Sonata op. 109, and Hindemith's Third Sonata. The response from the critics in Los Angeles was mixed. The *Los Angeles Herald-Examiner* found Gould's Beethoven "the ultimate of poetry and eloquence," while the *Los Angeles Times* reviewer deemed it "a misfortune throughout." There was nothing out of the ordinary about this particular concert, with the exception of one detail: It was the last concert Glenn Gould ever gave in public. He had another one scheduled for Minneapolis a week later, but at the last minute he canceled it.

At the age of thirty-one Gould, who commanded among the highest fees of any living pianist, retired from the concert stage, never to return. Edquist remembered the day CD 318 arrived home from Los Angeles, in a huge transportation crate that had been constructed just for that trip. "It was painted gray and looked like a battleship," he recalled. It took an extra couple of movers to uncrate the piano and move it up to the third-floor concert room. Edquist knew Gould spent an exorbitant sum to have the piano shipped to California and back for that concert, but he knew why: It was the only instrument Gould could rely on.

Gould made no public announcement of his decision to quit performing. He simply stopped. Critics gradually became aware of his absence. In late 1965, a *New York Times* critic wrote a piece under the headline "The Vanishing Glenn Gould." Gould, for his part, referred to 1965 as "a sabbatical year" and talked of perhaps giving concerts again in a few years. But he never did. Kevin Bazzana, the author of what is widely considered to be the definitive Gould biography, said he prefers to think that Gould simply drifted away from concerts, that he didn't explicitly quit on April 10, 1964, so much as gradually become aware that he would rather not go back.

Other pianists believed they understood. Gould was "just too sensitive to take part in the brutal competitiveness of concert-giving," Ivo Pogorelich, the Croatian pianist, once told an interviewer. "He was not a soldier, he was a very delicate personality." Gould once tried to convince Stephen Bishop-Kovacevich, who was several years younger than he, to stop playing in public, telling him it was "beneath him." And over the years, Bishop-Kovacevich said, he saw what he meant: "It takes only one person coughing, or turning the pages of a score, to ruin a passage," he said.

Gould decided that he would devote the rest of his career to recording. At around this time he wrote a letter to an acquaintance explaining that the microphone was a friend, not an enemy, and the lack of an audience, the total anonymity of the studio, "provides the greatest incentive to satisfy my demands upon myself without consideration for, or qualification by, the intellectual appetite, or lack of it, on the part of the audience."

Gould also decided that 318 was the piano he would use in all of his recording sessions. After he gave up performing in public, CD 318 was moved to Columbia Records' Thirtieth Street recording studio in New York City, where it remained, stowed away and locked in a corner, for the many years that Gould carried out his astonishing and groundbreaking recording career. CD 318 became known to everyone who worked at or passed through the studio as "the Gould piano," and it was tacitly understood that it should not be touched by anyone, under any circumstances.

When he wasn't recording in New York, Gould remained firmly planted in Toronto. He conducted much of his business from his agent's office, and was such a well-liked fixture at the Canadian Broadcasting Corporation that he was given an office of sorts there—a desk in a little-used corner of the music division. Beginning in the mid-1960s, he rented studio space in Toronto for the purpose of editing recordings and making radio programs. Over the years, it became a cluttered heap of papers, tape reels, scores, and recording equipment.

Gould's living and work spaces were in fact notoriously messy. He was in his late twenties when he finally moved out of his parents' house in 1959. After trying out different apartments, in 1960 he settled into a six-room penthouse at the Park Lane Apartments on Saint Clair Avenue West in a quiet neighborhood in midtown Toronto. Over the years, the apartment became an eyesore. Having grown up with maids and a doting mother, Gould had never been much of a housekeeper, and he had no talent for interior decoration. Because of his reclusive tendencies, few people ever went to his apartment, but those who did encountered something of a pigsty: plain, well-worn furniture—much of which had been left behind by the previous occupant—that had grown downright shabby over the years; stacks of papers that teetered as they grew; and so much miscellaneous clutter that the housecleaners he hired often simply threw up their hands and gave up. Nor was he much of a host. One friend who visited him for lunch was served hard, bland Arrowroot biscuits simply dumped from the box onto the sofa, and instant coffee made from hot tap water. In fact, when it came to food, he was unapologetically ascetic. He once said he was almost completely indifferent to eating and to the restaurant rituals that often accompany it: menus, wine lists, obsequious waiters, and endless dinner-table small talk. The only sustenance many of his friends saw him take were coffee, tea, and juice, and of course the Arrowroot biscuits, which he often munched on during recording sessions.

In the early 1960s, Edquist's visits to the Saint Clair apartment were few, as Gould seldom sought a tuning for the two pianos he played there on a daily basis—the Chickering and his seven-foot Steinway B. In fact, he was convinced that, mysteriously enough, the Steinway B never went out of tune. "I wish I had a simple explanation—or, indeed, any kind of an explanation—to account for this rather unusual phenomenon (if I did, I'd patent it)," he once wrote in a letter to the pianist Carol Montparker. "I am . . . quite used to skeptical glances and suggestions from friends that I have simply invented this improbable story and am probably smuggling in tuners under the cover of darkness."

It wasn't until 1968, after a three-year sabbatical from Eaton's during which he took an assistant manager's position at

Heintzman, that Verne Edquist started working in earnest on CD 318. By that time, Gould was bringing CD 318 up to Toronto for longer stretches and Edquist had developed a reputation as one of the best tuners in Toronto. ("His tuning is like gold," said one old hand.) Their first recording session together using CD 318 was for a CBC broadcast, and it gave Edquist a concentrated dose of all that lay in store for him with the famous pianist.

The session was to take place at an old theater that the CBC had been using as a recording studio. Edquist arrived early only to find the piano locked, which left him stranded for at least an hour, wasting good time he could have put to use tuning. When Gould finally showed up, he seemed surprised to see the tuner idle. Then, noticing that the piano was locked, he began to mutter to himself about not being able to find the key. Edquist was nonplussed but too tongue-tied to speak. Finally Gould pulled a key out of his pocket: "I guess I found it," he announced, and after unlocking it he went off for his hand-soaking ritual.

The work that Gould wanted Edquist to do, of course, was to lighten the action as much as possible. Gould insisted that the way to accomplish this was to reduce the key depth—the distance the key must travel from its position of rest to the place where it bottoms out on the front rail felt, or "punching." In other words: the amount the key must be depressed before the string sounds the note. But in fact, as Edquist knew, key depth—or key dip, or key travel, as it is often called—has nothing whatsoever to do with the sound. Edquist resisted at first, knowing that this would set off a domino effect: In order to reduce the key depth, he would have to change the blow distance of the hammers. Normally a hammer travels one and seven-eighths inches before it hits the strings, and Gould was in effect asking him to reduce that distance by several fractions of an inch. Gould argued that with the hammers closer to the strings, he would get what he called "a more immediate bite." But Edquist countered that the hammers travel that far for a reason: to give the piano power. Shorten the blow distance and you reduce the piano's dynamic range. But this was a sacrifice Gould was willing to make, and he wouldn't yield. He conceded that he was willing to give up a certain amount of total sound in exchange for what he called "more contrapuntal control." So Edquist went through the painstaking, multihour process of changing the key dip and blow distance on each of 318's eighty-eight hammers.

And if Edquist took shortcuts, or didn't adjust each hammer in precisely the same way, Gould noticed, because when it came to the tactile experience of playing the piano, there was little that escaped him. His fingertips were powerfully sensitive registers of distance, pressure, and resistance.

In short, Gould wanted to make 318 feel more like the Chickering. It was a vague mandate at best. Over the years, as Edquist tried one adjustment after another, he came to feel like a dog that was chasing its own tail.

As preternaturally gifted a musician as Gould was, he was still utterly dependent on the technician to keep 318 in top condition, which enabled him to fully achieve his distinct playing style. So it was that Edquist, the man who would tune, regulate, and modify the instrument according to Gould's unorthodox ideas—some of which horrified the traditionalists at Steinway—became almost as important to Gould as CD 318 itself.

For their part, Eaton's and Steinway—especially Steinway—were only too happy to let Gould do whatever he wanted to the piano, for they had long since written it off as over the hill. In fact, the folks at Steinway couldn't have asked for a happier outcome after the torturous years of struggle with this musician. And it was in the best of causes: 318 was to become an essential part of Gould's creative process, the means he used to express his interpretations of a select set of composers, most notably J. S. Bach.

When he played, Gould minimized use of the sustain pedal, relying instead on his fingers to produce a clean, detached sound that was reminiscent of a harpsichord. But when playing early music, he also often played with the soft pedal, which meant the hammer was hitting only two of the three strings, giving him a leaner sound. This further complicated Edquist's job, because when a piano is played this way it goes out of tune more quickly: The hammer is hitting two strings with the same intensity that it would normally hit three. Those two strings produce a sound with a thinner quality, and while this is what Gould was looking for, it meant that Edquist had to be on constant alert.

All of Edquist's tinkering eventually created an instrument that was so jittery it got what can only be described as the hiccups. After any pianist's finger hits a key, the wood-and-felt hammer flies at the string with a velocity determined by the speed with which the key has been struck. But the instant after the hammer sends the string vibrating, it must immediately return to a resting position so that it is ready for the pianist to hit it again. Gould's demand for hair-trigger action and lightning-fast repetition required an internal mechanism that was regulated into such a skittish state that occasionally the hammer would accidentally rebound from its resting place and strike the string again, producing an echo that sounded like an extra note. Oddly enough, Gould didn't seem to mind this quirk in 318. In fact, he started referring to the extra notes—the "hiccups"—as his "friends."

Once the piano was exactly as Gould wanted it, the hiccups became so ubiquitous that when Gould recorded the Bach *Inventions*, a CBS sound engineer had to work overtime to splice out the majority of the stray notes. Those that remained became the subject of a disclaimer that Gould wrote, which accompanied the liner notes. It was more of an homage to 318 than an excuse for all the extra notes: "Our enthusiasm for the rather extraordinary sound the piano now possessed allowed us to minimize the one minor aftereffect which it had sustained—a slight nervous tic in the middle register which in slower passages can be heard emitting a sort of hiccup. I must confess that I have grown somewhat accustomed to it. I now find this charming idiosyncrasy entirely worthy of the remarkable instrument which produced it." In the very first bars of the first piece on the record, the hiccups announce their presence.

An outstanding technician like Verne Edquist, who is highly attuned to a pianist's needs, is the hidden secret behind many an acclaimed performer. As his skill increased over the years, Edquist began to connect his work on pianos to the pianists who performed on them. He began to understand that when a tuner does his work well, the pianist is likely to perform better. And Glenn Gould was no exception.

Unlike the chilly relationship between Gould and Eaton's previous tuner, the outspoken George Cook, a strong and successful partnership took root between the brilliant pianist and the superb tuner. They were a dynamic team. Edquist not only had an unparalleled ear and extraordinary technical ability, but he also understood, at the deepest level, what it was that Gould was looking for, especially when it came to the all-important action.

Edquist tuned for many famous musicians over the years— Duke Ellington, Arthur Rubinstein, Rudolf Serkin, Victor Borge, even Liberace. And while Gould was never generous with his expressions of gratitude, Edquist knew, because Gould would go so far as to cancel a recording session unless Edquist could be there, that he appreciated his work. Still better, it was his work with Gould that eventually enabled Edquist to quit Eaton's employ and sustain his family for two decades as Gould's full-time private technician.

He took great pride in his work, and knew that he could do

something that was rare. And he was aware that even among piano tuners his hearing was especially acute. He detected such hairline differences in tones that sometimes it surprised even him. Over the years Edquist developed greater and greater confidence in his abilities, and when he thought something needed to be done to 318, he did it. One day, not long after he had started working full-time for Gould, Edquist arrived early to start tuning the piano for a CBC television program Gould was making. Edquist noticed that 318's keys were dirty, even slightly sticky, as if someone had smeared a light coat of jam on them. The tuner decided they needed to be cleaned. He got a few paper towels and some dish detergent and wiped them off, making them shiny and slick and, to Edquist's immense satisfaction, as good as new. But new wasn't what Gould wanted. When he arrived for the session, sat down at the piano, and started playing, he noticed immediately that the keys were different. He stopped, stood up, and asked Edquist what had happened to the keyboard. The rebuke Edquist received stung more for its tone than anything else. Gould snapped: "Don't do that again." Edquist felt like a small child who had, with the best of intentions, polished the silver with Ajax, only to be punished instead of rewarded. Still, Edquist understood and even respected Gould's reaction. He could see by now that this piano had become an extension of Gould himself, and the gummy keys, which Gould preferred to smooth ones, were a necessary part of the conduit between Gould's head and the sounds that emerged from the instrument. Edquist's job was to abet, not hinder, even if it defied common practice.

Gould had grown deeply fond of the instrument, battered and scarred as it was. Even though he didn't know precisely when the piano had been built, whenever someone asked how old it was—for indeed it looked ancient—he simply replied that CD 318 dated to the 1930s, that Steinway golden era between the two world wars. He seemed proud of the fact that his piano was "not quite Government Issue," as he put it, but close. He liked its shabby, down-at-the-heels appearance. But what Gould loved more than anything was the control he felt he had. The hair trigger on 318 was like a throttle on a race car. "It's a joy to play on, once you get the hang of it," Gould told an interviewer in 1968. "That takes a little time."

By the late 1960s, the hair-trigger action was so sensitive that the slightest depression sent the hammers flying at the strings. "We've put about seven years into refining certain qualities that it seemed to have natively, and to perfecting them along lines that seemed to me important if one's going to use the piano to peruse the Baroque repertoire, especially," he explained to an interviewer. "At one time, I found it important to have a different sort of piano for every kind of music that one played. I no longer do. I use it for everything now; it's my Richard Strauss piano, it's my Bach piano, it's my piano for playing William Byrd."

CD 318's tone was so versatile that Gould was convinced it could be made to sound orchestral. In 1967, before recording Beethoven's Fifth Symphony as arranged by Liszt, Edquist "sugarcoated" the hammers: Using short needles, he softened the very top few layers of felt on the crown, or strike point, of each one. Gould could then play very softly, conjuring corresponding orchestral instruments. But because only the top layer of the hammer felt was softened, he could still produce the sound of crashing cymbals with a forceful blow. "It has a lot of fat and fluffy sounds in that recording because we wanted it to sound that way," he told an interviewer. Gould could barely contain his delight with what 318 had become. "It's a chest of whistles, it's a set of virginals," he said. "It's just about anything that you want to make of it. It's an extraordinary piano."

SEVEN

CD 318 in the Studio

March 1963, Columbia Recording Studio, Thirtieth Street, Manhattan. Gould was happiest when in the studio, seated on his trusty chair. Photograph by Don Hunstein, courtesy of Sony BMG Music Entertainment.

From the start of his career, Gould adhered to a strongly held personal credo: If you have nothing new to say about a piece of music, don't play it, and certainly don't record it. If there are twenty terrific recordings of the Emperor Concerto, why bother to make a twenty-first if you don't have an interesting new interpretation to offer? His own choices were wide-ranging, and even if he didn't like a piece—for example, middle-period Beethoven like the Tempest Sonata and the Emperor Concerto—if he had something noteworthy to say, he recorded it.

To Gould, a recording was not intended to be a replica of—or indeed a replacement for—the concert experience. It was an art form of its own. He loved the liberating feeling he got when he entered the studio in "sixteen different minds" about how a piece should go and then observed his final opinion emerging only after several hours before the microphone. A live concert would never have given him the luxury of so many options. Also, in the studio Gould could employ what he called "editorial afterthought." Working in a predigital world, Gould was an outspoken defender of tape splicing, and he saw no reason why a musician shouldn't play a piece of music in 162 different segments.

Unlike many classical musicians, Gould became intimately involved in the postrecording process of splicing and mixing. The engineer would give him everything that he had recorded, and Gould would painstakingly pore over each take, deciding how the various pieces would be spliced together, which inserts would go where, and other sorts of audio manipulation such as the tweaking of the dynamic level of a phrase or a few notes—the electronic equivalent of applying makeup. The resulting whole was a distinct, unique interpretation sculpted from many parts. As he put the pieces together he wasn't necessarily correcting errors—partly because he rarely hit wrong notes—but actually shaping the interpretation of the piece itself. Eventually, although he did not physically splice the tapes himself, Gould came to understand tape splicing as well as a professional editor, and he came to be regarded as an artist of the studio for his technical astuteness and creativity as well as for his musical genius.

Indeed, Gould's decision to retreat into what he called the cloistered environment of the recording studio was not only inevitable, given his obsessions about travel and performance, but also suited him perfectly as an artist. "When you are making a recording you are left alone," he once told an interviewer. "You're not surrounded by five hundred, five thousand, fifty thousand people who are in a position to say, 'Aha! That's what he thinks of that work, eh?'"

The bulk of Gould's output—more than ninety recordings of hundreds of works—was made on CD 318. With that piano's keys under his fingers, he swept through an astonishingly diverse repertoire that included Beethoven, Liszt, Strauss, and a number of modern composers including Schoenberg, Hindemith, Prokofiev, and Scriabin. But the heart of his recording oeuvre was the works of J. S. Bach. And for playing Bach, the recording studio was precisely where he believed he needed to be. What was involved intellectually in playing Bach's music required superhuman concentration. Playing virtuosic Liszt can be more difficult in the sense that it requires more bravura, but such music also gives a pianist places to hide. The perfect striking of every single note isn't necessary, because in the presence of so *many* notes and loud, bold, chordal structures, even the most astute listener was unlikely to miss a single note or two. But to play Bach the way Gould did required that every note be

perfectly articulated at all times. It is music that, as Kevin Bazzana put it, "is ruthlessly exposed from beginning to end. You
can't fudge or fake anything in Bach."

Carol Montparker agreed. Bach's music, she once wrote, is
"fragile, tenuous and so pure that the slightest flaw becomes
magnified a hundredfold." It was no wonder, to Montparker
and many others, that Gould preferred to make his music in the
privacy of the sound studio—that he chose "to keep his superb
Bach from the rigors of public performance in favor of recording . . . When the artist is too vulnerable, he should, ideally, be
placed in a soundproof booth . . . No matter how minute the
imperfection, it is that which lingers on to haunt and harass,
obliterating all the good stuff."

Gould's Bach recordings in particular, wrote the critic Harold
Schonberg, "forced professionals, music lovers and critics to re-
consider the music, throwing overboard all preconceived notions." It was not just that Gould had wonderful fingers,
Schonberg wrote. When he created his Bach recordings, Gould
made the music sound different: in tempo, in phrase, in dynamics, in conception. "Elements nobody had paid much attention
to in the past suddenly sprang into high relief."

A good deal of the freshness Gould brought to each recording was due, he believed, to his instrument. This was true not
just of the Bach he played on 318 but also of Orlando Gibbons,
especially the brief "Italian Ground," in which Gould's fingers
skated across the keyboard. When Gould played Gibbons on
318, it became a perfect convergence of pianist, composer,
tuner, and instrument, as if all roads had led to that one complete musical moment.

A new Gould album was always an important musical event,
so much so that at times it didn't seem to matter what he decided to play. "You are one of the few authentic geniuses recording today," Peter Munves, the director of classical music at

Columbia's rival RCA Records, wrote to Gould. "If you wanted to record the complete works of Alban Berg on a kazoo, I'd gladly do it."

When Gould was around 318, he guarded the piano with his life. "He talked about his piano as if it were human," fellow pianist David Bar-Illan commented. "He talked of its temperaments. He was proud of it. His piano, he said, improved with age." Bar-Illan recalled that he once played on CD 318 in New York—with Gould's permission, of course. It was a virtuosic piece, and as he raised his hand high, in preparation to play a large chord, Gould suddenly lurched forward, thinking Bar-Illan was about to come down hard on the instrument, and cried out, "Oh, no, no! Don't! Don't! Wait!"

Edquist recalled a similar instance that took place before a recording session. He had just tuned 318 and then had, somewhat absentmindedly, run his hand along the piano's cast-iron plate, much as a groom might stroke a horse after a grooming. Gould saw this and said, only half in jest, "Look, but don't touch."

Gould knew, of course, that 318 needed to be constantly tuned and regulated, and for years he relied on a small but carefully chosen circle of technicians. Edquist was by no means the only tuner who worked on the cherished piano. Ted Sambell, a talented Canadian technician, tuned the piano frequently in the early 1960s before Edquist returned from his stint at Heintzman. And when the piano was in the New York studio for long stretches of time, Gould relied on Franz Mohr, Steinway's chief concert tuner after Bill Hupfer. Sometimes Gould even asked Mohr to come to Toronto to tend to 318 without telling Edquist. In fact, when it came to his tuners, Gould was like a bigamist who invested great care and energy into keeping his families in different cities, making certain they didn't discover one another's existence. Gould was skilled at making each man think he was the only technician in his life. He did this in much the way he consulted different doctors about various ailments, usually failing to inform each one of the others' diagnoses or prescriptions. In this way Gould succeeded in staying well stocked in medication and physiological caretakers. Perhaps not surprisingly, he accorded the same care—and discretion—to the piano he loved so dearly.

A German immigrant who had served his apprenticeship as a concert technician in Düsseldorf, Franz Mohr arrived in New York in 1962, encouraged by a vice-consul at the American embassy in Frankfurt who had told him, "The whole country is out of tune. You'd better come." He was hired sight unseen by a Steinway desperate for good tuners.

Once at Steinway, Mohr spent much of his time in the service of Vladimir Horowitz, whose personal Steinway he spent years refining to the maestro's specifications. Gould admired Mohr not only because he fully appreciated what Gould valued in a piano, but also because he had an uncanny understanding of how to get at it as a technician. "It takes time to convey what I want, because I don't have a strong mechanical sense, but Franz is a wonderfully observant man who sits sometimes and watches you play for half an hour and then says, 'Aha. I see that's what you like to play, and therefore what you're probably complaining about is . . .'"

Mohr was a deeply religious Christian who found his faith one epiphanous night while still a teenager, and as an adult he became something of a Johnny Bibleseed. Mohr tried to make a believer out of Arthur Rubinstein, who dismissed him with characteristic levity. "Don't worry about me, Franz. When I get to heaven, I have no problem. I am Jewish, and if Moses is there at the gate, he will let me in. You know my wife is Catholic—maybe it is Saint Peter who is at the gate. So he will let me in. And I have a son-in-law who is an Episcopalian minister—so how can I lose!"

Mohr's attempts to help Glenn Gould get religion, however, were met with less humor. Gould was extremely superstitious; he was fascinated by religion as an otherworldly phenomenon, but in the same way that he was intrigued by extrasensory perception and telepathy—and he tuned out Mohr's religious admonitions. Mohr, for his part, was oblivious and insisted, years later, that Gould's appreciation for Scripture, especially as expressed through Bach's cantatas, was proof of the pianist's religious leanings.

Among Mohr's other strongly held beliefs was the conviction that he was Gould's only tuner. "Over the years I earned his trust; he would not let anyone touch [CD 318] but me," Mohr wrote in a 1992 memoir. It was an odd statement, to be sure, for Mohr traveled seldom to Toronto, where 318 spent much of its life. Perhaps Mohr thought that, when in Toronto, the piano tuned itself.

Edquist likewise heard little about other tuners. Gould succeeded in making each of his technicians feel special and uniquely responsible for 318's well-being.

AFTER MORE THAN a dozen years of commuting to Manhattan for recording sessions at CBS, in the late 1960s Gould decided to move his recording operation—and CD 318—to the Eaton Auditorium in Toronto, which was a few minutes' drive from his apartment. Music critics dismissed the Eaton space for the poor quality of its acoustics, but Gould preferred it to any other setting partly because, in typical contrarian style, he liked the hall's acoustics. And, of course, it was familiar: He had played there as a child.

Gould paid to have 318 shipped up from New York permanently, and a new phase of his career began. The arrangement was ideal. Instead of taking a seven-hour train or car trip to New

York, Gould now traveled less than a mile downtown to Eaton's. His faithful producer at CBS Masterworks, Andrew Kazdin, began flying up to Toronto for marathon recording sessions that lasted two or three days at a time. And Gould discovered a highly talented sound engineer named Lorne Tulk, a patient young man and master splicer, who would soon become a close friend. The final member of the team was Ray Roberts, a loyal worker who became Gould's Man Friday: He kept Gould's cars in good working condition, handled logistics, and set up and took down the equipment for the recording sessions. Over the next several years, these men would spend hundreds of nocturnal hours together in an empty penthouse auditorium, creating some of the most memorable classical-piano recordings of the twentieth century.

At first Gould complained about the sound coming from the piano. He described it as "cluttered." Together, Gould, Kazdin, and Edquist searched for the cause. After a lengthy process of elimination, they decided there was something about the interaction of CD 318's body, its curved front lip, and the lid that was creating the acoustic congestion Gould was hearing. Kazdin had an idea: remove the lid and raise the microphones so they pointed down toward the exposed cast-iron frame and soundboard. It worked, and Gould was delighted.

Finally suited to its unique setting, 318 produced a singular sound, and the recordings had a warm, comfortable acoustic. Eaton Auditorium became the location for Gould's most prolific recording period, the place he recorded prodigious amounts of Bach as well as Grieg, Sibelius, Beethoven, Haydn, Scriabin, and Bizet—all of it on CD 318.

The piano wasn't the only thing Gould was attuned to. Even while playing, he could sense if there was someone else in the auditorium. Perhaps it was the way the sound of a human body changed the delicate balance of acoustics in the room, or perhaps he could hear a shuffle or a breath. Whatever it was, no one else would hear a thing. On these occasions Gould would suddenly stop playing and ask Kazdin or Roberts to search the auditorium for interlopers. And he was right every time. The stowaway (usually a shoplifter, hiding on the floor between the rows) would be escorted down to security, and recording would resume.

For someone so sensitive to noise, Gould was unbothered by some of the stray sounds that ended up in his recordings. His engineers grappled with a full complement of extraneous noises. There was the vocal accompaniment and the now-famous hiccups. And of course the chair, which creaked and snapped incessantly as it swung and swayed. It was precisely this weaving back and forth and side to side that Gould found indispensable to his playing, and no amount of lubrication seemed to help the noise. The engineers tried to remove as many of the nonmusical vocalizations as possible, but there was only so much they could do, and the chorus of sounds on a Gould recording became something of a signature of his work.

As Kevin Bazzana observed, "This does seem odd for someone who fussed so much—interpretively, digitally, mechanically—in order to get the most pristine performances out of himself. Odd that he wouldn't mind if those performances were, to some ears, ruined by his own croaking or his squeaky chair, whereas an ambient sound from a studio technician, say, would have been unacceptable."

WHEN THEY WERE recording together, Gould's team fell into a routine, a circadian rhythm that was dictated partly by Gould, who seldom started his day before midafternoon, and partly by the schedule at Eaton's, which was, after all, a busy and noisy department store that rang with the sounds of rising and falling elevators, cash registers, opening and closing doors, and the general hum and bustle of the hundreds of customers who passed through its aisles every day. So Gould and his team began their recording sessions only after the store had closed for the day. This put the group to work some time after eight P.M. and kept them there well into the early morning.

Edquist, Ray Roberts, Lorne Tulk, and Andrew Kazdin usually arrived a few hours before the session was to start. Roberts, ever mindful of Gould's obsession with germs, would spray disinfectant on all the furniture and equipment that he knew Gould would come into contact with. Then he and Tulk would set up the three seven-and-a-half-foot-tall microphones, placing them strategically around the piano, fifteen to twenty feet away, between two rows of seats. And of course someone always placed the blocks under each of the piano's three legs to bring it to the precise height—in relation to the pygmy chair—that Gould required.

Edquist arrived early to tune the piano. After another hour or so, by about nine P.M., Gould would show up. The tap water in the Eaton's lavatory was not hot enough for his crucial hand-soaking ritual, so he had Roberts bring in an electric tea kettle. Thirty minutes before he sat down to play, the kettle would be switched on, the hot water poured into the lavatory sink, and Gould would excuse himself to "go soak."

The first thing Gould did was sit down and record what was known as an "overall" or "basic" take, running through the entire piece. He then went to the control room to listen. More often than not, Gould would decide to record more than one basic take; he would then listen to them all and decide which one would become the master take. While listening, he would make notes on the score, noting where he believed changes were required. The rest of the session was spent working on the changes, which became inserts in the master take.

To make the fixes, the passages immediately leading up to the points that needed to be changed were played back to Gould through a speaker beside the piano. This gave him the chance to hear the color and texture and to get the precise tempo. Then, when the bar or note that needed to be replaced was reached, the playback was stopped and he would immediately play the insert. Once Gould had played the repair patch to his liking, the group moved on to the next one. Later the fixes were edited into a composite tape.

Throughout a session, he spent a lot of time shuttling between 318 and the control room. Whenever Gould was away from the piano, Edquist would seize the opportunity to touch it up. Standing there, listening to Gould play, Edquist could actually hear the piano go out of tune under the pianist's fingers. Like parents attuned to the slightest mood shift in their infant, the two men paid minute attention to any changes in the piano's tone. In fact, they even grew slightly competitive about being the first to hear when CD 318 was going out of tune. Edquist took special pride in his quick auditory reflex. He could tell when a tone was starting to "curl," and invariably it was he who caught it first. But he often said nothing until, a minute or so later, Gould heard it too, stopped in the middle of a take, and asked Edquist to fix it. Similarly, once or twice every session, often in the middle of a long night of recording, perhaps even in the middle of a phrase, Gould would suddenly decide that 318 needed voicing. All activity would come to a halt while Edquist slid the action out of the piano and went to work on the hammer felts.

During breaks, Gould liked to have a cup of coffee: a strong cup with two sugars and extra cream, which he called a "double double." Inevitably it was Edquist who was sent off to Fran's, an all-night coffee shop around the corner, for the coffee and a "Franburger"—tomatoes, relish, and no onion—for Kazdin.

Sometimes, when he was feeling bold, Edquist tried to talk Gould out of it. Coffee, he told him, wasn't healthy in the first place, but double cream and double sugar? The pianist shrugged the advice off. Edquist knew he had a time limit, perhaps fifteen or twenty minutes while Gould and Kazdin reviewed the tapes, and he tried to go quickly. One night, Edquist was near the entrance to Fran's when he came upon a vicious dog barking at him in attack mode. "Some hippie had tied his dog to the door," Edquist recalled. "But I thought, Well, I'm more afraid of Glenn than I am of the dog, so I pushed him aside and went in."

Edquist found that he was no match for Gould's infinite energy during those late-night recording sessions. Particularly when Gould spent hours doing take after take of composers Edquist had trouble even comprehending, such as Schoenberg, Edquist would frequently fall asleep from exhaustion. "He looked at me once, and I was sleeping on the set, and he said, 'You must be the most relaxed tuner in the world,'" Edquist once recalled. By the third night of a recording marathon, Edquist would be running on fumes.

Something about the unorthodox hours and the unconventional venue made the nocturnal crew seem less like technicians at a recording session than like congregants in a witch's coven, conjuring spirits from the vast deep of the musical canon and capturing them on tape. Over and over again.

When he finished a session, drenched with sweat from the energy he had expended, Gould would disappear to change his shirt, and then reemerge. But instead of putting on his hat and coat, he would sit back down at the piano and play whatever came into his head: a show tune like "Some Enchanted Evening," or a jazz standard like Duke Ellington's "Caravan." "It just rolled out of him," Edquist observed, but it wasn't only Gould: It was the piano as well. There was a lot more sound than usual coming out of CD 318, perhaps because Gould, ordinarily very sparing in his use of the sustain pedal, would put it to full use when he was playing, or riffing on, popular music—and he also used more keys than he needed for Bach, thereby realizing the full potential of the instrument. "It was a house full of piano," Edquist said. "Every note was almost resonating with every chord. It was times like that when I called the piano a harmonic fountain." It was in those playful postsession moments that Gould was at his most relaxed.

When a session finally wound down, often as late as four A.M., after CD 318's fallboard had been padlocked and the microphones, stands, power supplies, and tape recorders had been broken down and packed up, a peculiar routine unfolded. Gould paid each man—Kazdin, Roberts, Tulk, Edquist—with a personal check. But after writing each check, he would scrutinize it for a moment to determine if it was lucky or unlucky. It could be any number of things that made a check unlucky: the number, the way he had signed his name, or the level of dexterity with which he had written it. But more often than not, it was simply the *feeling* he got from the check at hand. If he got a bad feeling and decided it was unlucky, he would announce, "I don't think I like this one." Instead of ripping it up, he would tuck it away somewhere and write a new one. Once, after writing what he had decided was an acceptable check to Kazdin, he later called the producer in his hotel to say that what Kazdin had in his possession was in fact an unlucky check. He apologized at length and promised he would drop off a replacement check at the hotel.

Superstition and fear were at the root of many of Gould's actions and behaviors. He disliked giving autographs for the same reason he was wary of writing checks: for fear the results might be unlucky. But when he did give an autograph or sign a check (or any other document, for that matter), he always misspelled his own first name, writing it as "Glen." Kazdin once asked him why, and Gould explained that he had discovered years earlier that once he got his hand to start forming the two *n*'s he couldn't stop and would keep going and write three, so he decided to abort the exercise after one. Kazdin was skeptical. "This supposed lack of manual control is a little hard to swallow coming from the man who could play an unbroken stream of thirty-second notes faster and cleaner than any other pianist on the face of the earth," Kazdin wrote in an acerbic memoir about Gould, titled *Glenn Gould at Work: Creative Lying.*

Although Gould had long since completely given up performing, and recorded exclusively in Toronto, he still received requests to record popular concerto works. In 1971 he decided to rerecord Beethoven's Second Concerto, this time in stereo, as well as the Grieg Concerto, which marked a true departure for him, as it was precisely the kind of Romantic music no one would have expected him to play. He chose the Cleveland Orchestra to accompany him. Not only was Cleveland arguably the best orchestra in America at the time, but Gould had always loved it. And, conveniently enough, they were under contract to Columbia Records.

But Gould didn't love the concert grands available in Cleveland. So arrangements were made for CD 318 to be shipped to Ohio. He knew Edquist would be reluctant to make the trip, so he wrote to Steinway asking for the services of Franz Mohr. In early 1971 he had sent the piano down to New York for minor repairs and reported his delight with the results to David Rubin.

> CD 318 is, I'm happy to say, restored to its glories as of yore. We've now done six sessions on it and, if anything, it sounds better each time out. Franz did a superb job of restoration and I would ask you to let him know how very pleased I am

about it. Whatever the secret of his ministrations I trust he
will patent them since, even though with our new Toronto-
bound policy, life is simplified enormously, there will be still
occasions when 318 will have to hit the road and that, as you
know, is usually when trouble begins. The only such occasion
in the near future is next September when I'll be recording
with the Cleveland Orchestra. I think I mentioned those dates
to you some time ago and expressed the hope at that time that
Franz could stand by in Cleveland for the opening sessions.

Mohr was too busy to go to Cleveland, however, so Gould
talked Edquist into making the trip.

All the arrangements were made, and Columbia Records prepared to ship the recording equipment to Cleveland. Just before
the session dates, 318 was packed into its crate, put on a truck,
and shipped to Severance Hall in Cleveland. Edquist and Kazdin
got their plane tickets, and Ray Roberts prepared to drive to
Cleveland with Gould, who had long since sworn off flying,
which had by now become a source of paralyzing fear.

Then, just as everyone was set to leave, Gould suddenly canceled the recording. He had come down with a cold, he claimed.
The pianist was famously capricious when it came to fulfilling
professional obligations, and the actual reason could have been
almost anything. He might have been worried about catching a
cold once he arrived in Cleveland, or disliked the idea of sitting
in a drafty concert hall for an extended period. He might have
had an aversion to the five-hour car trip. He might even have
had misgivings about playing something so out of character as
the Grieg.

Gould's cancellation of the Cleveland trip caused considerable inconvenience. Not only had an entire orchestra been
booked, but the piano had been sent 250 miles for nothing.
Executives at Columbia Records were furious, as they were now

on the hook to pay the Cleveland musicians for the missed session. But a deal was worked out whereby no charge would be made if Gould agreed to rebook the recording session for some time in the months to follow. And he did. But he didn't want 318 languishing in Cleveland, so he asked that the piano be shipped back to Toronto.

The piano was shipped back to Toronto in the same manner—by truck—that it had traveled to Cleveland, and it arrived a few weeks after the canceled session, just in time for a recording date at Eaton Auditorium. The night of the first recording session, Edquist went to the auditorium to get CD 318 tuned and ready. Casually he hit middle C, and was immediately taken aback: It was an entire octave too high. Hitting a few more notes confirmed that something was terribly wrong. He decided to lift the lid to make a proper diagnosis. But even that proved difficult, as it had gone out of alignment. He turned on as many lights as he could and trained his thick glasses on the cast-iron plate. To his astonishment, he found that it was cracked. There could be only one explanation. The worst had happened. Somewhere between Cleveland and Toronto, the piano had been dropped.

EIGHT

Broken Piano

Trying out pianos in the Steinway Basement in 1958. Gould with Fritz Steinway (with leg up) and two other Steinway & Sons employees. Photograph by Don Hunstein, courtesy of Sony BMG Music Entertainment.

EDQUIST MAY HAVE BEEN mostly blind, but there was no mistaking the tangled wreckage that CD 318 had become. The piano's previous dents and battle scars were insignificant compared to the condition it was in now. Merely dinged before, the lid was now completely twisted out of alignment and split apart at the bass end, its hinges horribly bent.

Edquist carefully removed the lid and peered inside, feeling with his fingertips. Then he crawled beneath the piano and, by touching the underside of the soundboard, could tell that it was split at the treble end. This meant that the thirteen-hundred-pound piano hadn't just slipped an inch or two. To receive such a gaping crack, it must have suffered a huge impact. It must, Edquist concluded, have plummeted at least several feet. Edquist also detected several cracks in the two-inch-thick keybed. It seemed that on impact, the action had shot forward several inches, taking with it the key blocks as well as a number of heavy screws and the dowels that held them in place. In its path, the runaway action had mowed down the key slip—the long, narrow, vertical strip of wood pinned to the front of the keybed—which was now pushed out and twisted.

But what shocked Edquist the most during his inspection was a large crack in the piano's iron plate, a 350-pound mass that is strong enough to carry twenty tons of string tension. When a piece of metal holding that much tension breaks, it would create an explosive sound that would rival a cannon firing. It was impossible, Edquist knew, that anyone present could fail to hear the combined noise of the piano falling and the plate exploding, so he presumed that the only people present at the loading dock were the crew of movers—three, maybe four men from Maislin or Robertson's, the local companies Eaton's hired for piano transport. Clearly they were alone at the dock and, rather than call the accident to anyone's attention, they had simply hoisted the piano, still in its crate, back to the spot from which it had fallen off the dock, taken it into the freight elevator, uncrated it, rolled it into the auditorium, set it up at the foot of the stage, and gotten the hell out of there. And to Edquist, that was the oddest part: The piano had simply been left as if nothing had happened, propped in place like an inconvenient corpse. The movers must have hoped no one would notice.

This wasn't the first time Edquist had seen a piano after a disaster. He had been asked to work on instruments that had been left outdoors in freezing temperatures, which causes the metal plate to grow brittle and, on rare occasions, even crack. But he had never seen anything quite like this. The extent of the damage to CD 318 was so extraordinary, Edquist recalled feeling that it was almost as if someone had committed intentional violence on it. Most worrisome of all, though, was the prospect of breaking the news to Gould. Edquist's first thought was like a child's reflexive relief at not being at fault. His next thought was that he didn't want to have to be the one to tell Gould what had happened.

As the evening wore on, others began to filter in for the night's recording session. Roberts began to unload the equipment, but Edquist told him not to bother because there wasn't going to be any recording that night. Andrew Kazdin and Lorne Tulk showed up shortly thereafter. Dolefully, the four men clustered around the damaged instrument. As they examined it more closely, they discovered that the cast-iron plate was cracked in not one but four places. It was then that someone raised the question: What to do? Should someone go to Gould's apartment, ring the bell, and break the news as if CD 318 were a fallen soldier? Should they just wait until he arrived at the auditorium? They agreed that Gould had to see the piano for himself, but that

he ought to be forewarned with a telephone call. After some discussion it was decided that Edquist, who knew the piano and its
passionate owner best, should be the one to make the call. An
hour later, Gould arrived at the auditorium in a state of unexpected calm. He walked up to the piano, took a brief look at the
keyboard, and, without so much as touching a key, said, "Can't
play on that."

He told everyone they could leave; there was no work to do.
Feeling an extra measure of responsibility, Edquist stayed behind with the pianist and his broken instrument. Once he was
alone with Edquist, Gould grew more agitated. Together they
went over what might have happened. "He grilled me like a
lawyer," Edquist recalled. After a few minutes it was clear that
there were too many questions, and neither man had answers.

The first thing Edquist did the next morning was go to the
Eaton's loading dock to examine the packing crate the piano
had been shipped in. He found a deep gouge on the left-hand
side near the top, and discovered that the wood block inside the
case, which was used as a brace, had been torn loose by the
force of the crash. Edquist then went upstairs to see Muriel
Mussen, who coordinated the comings and goings of Eaton's
concert grands. It came as no surprise to Edquist when she told
him she knew nothing of the accident. Yes, she said, it was
Robertson's that had delivered the piano, but no, they had reported nothing to her. When Edquist described to Mussen the
extent of the damage, she expressed shock and sympathy. She
knew how Gould had plucked the old, rejected, homely CD 318,
Cinderella-like, from backstage in the auditorium, how he had
come to love it, and how he and Edquist had spent years modifying it to perfection. She could only imagine the anguish Gould
must have been feeling.

Yet Gould, for his part, maintained an almost eerie calm. If
he was devastated, he did not show it. Almost immediately he

seemed resigned to the irreparable state of the piano. Soon after the accident, in a letter to David Rubin at Steinway, he was referring to the piano as if speaking of a beloved family member whose resuscitation no one had bothered to attempt.

The letter to Rubin laid out the damage in clinical detail:

> *The piano was apparently dropped with great force and the point of impact would appear to be the front right (treble) corner.*
>
> *The plate is fractured in four critical places.*
>
> *The lid is split at the bass and there is also considerable damage to it toward the treble end as well.*
>
> *The sounding board is split at the treble end.*
>
> *Key slip pins are bent out of line and the force of the impact was great enough to bend No. 10 type screws as well.*
>
> *The force was also great enough to put the key frame and action completely out of alignment, i.e., forward at the treble end.*

Gould wrote, "I am sure that these details will be substantially borne out by your technical people when they have a chance to assess the damage."

Yet for all his attempts at pragmatism, inwardly Gould was bereft. He was determined to find out who was responsible for destroying the piano, and he decided to sleuth the episode out for himself.

Robertson's, the moving firm, had a good reputation. Like Muriel Mussen before him, Gould could find no accident report in relation to any portion of the piano's journey back from Cleveland. It seemed to be the piano-moving equivalent of a hit and run. "While it was possible that whoever dropped the piano failed to appreciate the degree of internal damage which such a fall would cause," he wrote to Rubin, "I think the external damage alone to the case would be more than sufficient to have warranted a report of some kind."

He consulted with Mussen to gather details about the time and means of the piano's transport. According to her records, CD 318 had been crated on September 17, 1971, picked up by Maislin Transport, and trucked to Cleveland. More than a month later, when the piano was en route back to Toronto, Robertson's picked it up from "the Dump," the nickname for the customs shed on the outskirts of the city.

It was the return trip that most interested Gould. He pieced together a timeline, and discovered that the piano had undergone a trip so slow, it might have arrived in Toronto from the Canadian border more quickly had someone rolled it down the street. According to Mussen's records, the piano reached the border on October 13, three weeks after leaving Cleveland, via a trucking company called Intercity Transport. It arrived at the Dump the following day. That made some sense. What didn't, at least to Gould, was that it took three days for CD 318 to clear customs—where it was presumably uncrated and inspected—and then another two days for Robertson's to take it the few miles from the customs shed to the delivery ramp at Eaton's. It was not installed in the auditorium until October 26, nearly a week after arriving at Eaton's.

Gould found parts of this chronicle intriguing—and suspicious. In a letter to Steinway a few weeks after the accident he wrote: "The most obvious query would relate to the fact that it took them six days (admittedly counting a weekend) to move the piano from the ground floor to the seventh-floor auditorium; I also find it odd that it would require two days after customs clearance to go from the suburbs to the downtown store. I would ask that you handle these latter bits of information, or more accurately my paranoid suspicions in regard to them, with your customary discretion, but I'm sure you will agree that both questions could stand some elucidation."

It could be that Gould had just never paid much attention to the logistics of moving pianos from one city to another. And why should he have? His interest in piano moving heretofore began and ended with seeing the instrument properly situated on a stage or in the studio. Still, when he went over the timeline with Muriel Mussen, she agreed that CD 318's journey home from Cleveland had been tortuously slow.

Piano moving is an inherently tricky business. In cities filled with multistory apartment buildings with impossibly small elevators or narrow stairwells, pianos are often hoisted in the air, attached by reinforced steel cables, and moved by crane through a living room window. Nine-foot grand pianos have been moved in hotel elevators not inside the elevator car but on top of it, tied to the cable. The task of moving a piano, especially one as large, heavy, and oddly shaped as a concert grand, involves such challenging geometry that it has inspired its own mathematical puzzle, known as the Piano Mover's Problem. Robotics researchers in particular were intrigued by what they called a "motion-planning" problem that arises regularly in robotics, where the goal is to find an algorithm for moving a solid polyhedron (piano) from a given starting point to a given end point without colliding with a region bounded by impenetrable and immovable solid objects (walls, doorways, stairwells). In real life the apprenticeship of a piano mover is lengthy, and the level of confidence in an apprentice needs to be very high before he is allowed to move a piano, especially a grand, unsupervised. The crew from Robertson's was acknowledged to be among the best, and several of the movers at the company had moved nothing but pianos for years. The Robertson's crew had transported thousands of pianos under circumstances far more difficult than these.

Trying to make sense of what had happened, Gould focused on forensics. From the way the piano was damaged, it was obvious that it had tumbled headfirst. The specific loading dock that the piano arrived at was about five feet high, which would account for the force of the impact. It was also clear from the damage to the crate that the piano had been dropped before it was taken out of the crate. The accident could have happened as it was coming off the truck if the length of the crate exceeded the length of the truck lift. If the skid was longer than the lift gate, at some point it would protrude over the edge. With formidable weight come problems of balance and inertia. Moving a grand piano requires not just strength but constant communication. Good piano movers are always talking to each other in short, gruff bursts: "I'm there," and "One, two, go!" and "You take the top side," and "To you!" and "Watch the balance." Toronto's best movers—the crews sent out by Maislin and Robertson's—were so experienced, so accustomed to the demands of these tasks, that they became second nature. But inexperienced movers can easily forget that two thirds of a grand piano's weight is concentrated at the front of the instrument, producing a center of gravity so biased toward one end that perfect balance is essential—so much so that a moment's inattention can result in disaster.

Gould believed it was unlikely that professional piano movers had dropped CD 318. It was far more likely, he concluded, that the culprits had instead been Eaton's employees who worked with shipments leaving and arriving at the loading dock but who had no particular expertise in moving concert grands on and off the large vans. Typically, the movers delivered a piano as far as the loading dock, then left it for the Eaton's crew to take it to its final destination, which for CD 318 was the auditorium. And in the end, this was Robertson's claim: The moving company delivered the piano to the loading dock and after that, somehow, it fell, or was dropped or knocked off the edge.

Not long afterward, a story circulated that someone who was

inside Eaton's at the time saw the stage manager rushing out of his office and, when asked what was wrong, heard him reply, "We just dropped a piano!" Later this individual denied having uttered those words. "It was a third-party story at best," Ray Roberts said many years later. "You're not going to go to court with that."

Eventually, no doubt frustrated by the dead ends he kept encountering, Gould dropped his investigation. Over the years, when telling interviewers about the accident, he pointed no fingers, saying only that it happened at a loading dock, and that for him it was a tragic incident. He was right to let it go. Even if he had managed to figure out who was responsible, there would have been no way to prove it. And in the end, did it really matter? The damage had been done. The question for Gould became, Where to go from here?

NINE

Making Do

Gould at the wheel in April 1974. A famously bad driver, he once remarked, "It's true that I've driven through a number of red lights on occasion, but on the other hand I've stopped at a lot of green ones but never gotten credit for it." Photograph by Don Hunstein, courtesy of Sony BMG Music Entertainment.

After the accident, Gould started referring to the piano as "the late and very much lamented CD 318." Well into 1972, nearly a year after it had been dropped, Gould was telling friends and fellow musicians that CD 318 was, in all probability, damaged beyond repair, and he began toying with the idea of a replacement.

He knew that he couldn't fruitfully confine his search to the small stable of concert grands at Eaton's. At the same time, he had little desire to travel to the Steinway Basement in New York to play the pianos there. Over the years, especially after he stopped performing, he had grown more reclusive, and was increasingly traumatized by change. He had spent his entire life in the city where he was born, lived in his parents' house until he was nearly thirty, and for years used the same stockbroker, accountant, lawyer, and agent. He had sat on the same chair for nearly twenty years and played on the same piano for ten. The idea of switching to an entirely new piano was hard enough. But to spend hours on the road, to and from New York, in the course of such a switch seemed too much to ask.

Arguing that he would need an extended period in which to try out the most promising candidates, Gould wrote to Steinway & Sons and audaciously requested that the firm ship pianos to Toronto, preferably two at a time. Meanwhile he began thinking aloud about the possibility of cannibalizing CD 318 for its best bits. "I am most anxious to know whether any parts are salvageable and could be used in conjunction with another instrument," he wrote to Steinway's David Rubin. "It may be possible," he conjectured, "to salvage the action of this instrument but, if so, it would be installed within the chassis of another piano." But regardless of what happened with CD 318, he wanted Steinway to begin sending him their best pianos, in the hope that he would find an instrument that, he noted with some understatement, "comes closest to meeting my requirements."

Gould's elaborate fantasies notwithstanding, executives at Steinway & Sons were not inclined to start sending pianos up to Toronto, and turned down his request. Suddenly Gould grew sentimental about CD 318. All talk of giving up on the piano, or eviscerating it, vanished. He decided to ship CD 318 to New York to have technicians at Steinway work on it.

No one was particularly surprised. Gould forged his longest-lasting attachments with inanimate objects: his rattle-trap of a chair, his cars (he even named them), his fingerless gloves. Over the years, he had made sincere proclamations of his affection for CD 318 and would play on no other instrument. Now, at the hands of movers who were at best inattentive, at worst incompetent, the entire investment in 318 had come to a premature and abrupt end. It was a haunting and eerie reminder of what had happened fourteen years earlier to CD 174, another favorite piano that had been dropped on its way back from Cleveland, a city that was beginning to seem cursed.

Any objective outsider would have told Gould that the piano could be restored, but that it would never be returned to its original condition. And it most certainly would not be the piano he and Edquist had spent so many years turning into exactly the instrument he wanted, with the fluid action and regulation customized to his idiosyncratic needs. He knew this, of course. But he was unwilling, in the end, to turn his back on 318. When he called Muriel Mussen to ask her to arrange for the piano's trip to

New York, he made a bleak joke about tossing a coin to decide which mover she should call.

While waiting for CD 318 to return from New York, Gould decided to capitalize on the piano's absence and spend some time making a recording on the harpsichord. For years he had been interested in taping Handel's suites for harpsichord. He had originally planned to play them on 318, on which he had recorded so many other works, especially Bach, that had been written for the harpsichord. But with 318 out of commission, he decided to distract himself by playing and recording on an actual harpsichord. After all, he had managed to have 318 tweaked to the point where it nearly *was* a harpsichord, and a great deal of his playing simulated the sound of the piano's predecessor. Gould was intrigued by the harpsichord not only because it was the instrument Bach composed on but because it produced the sound Bach would have heard, clean and free of harmonic resonance. And it was precisely this clean, pure sound that Gould found appealing when playing Bach—and which he had tried to approach with CD 318 when, holding down the soft pedal, he used just two strings for each note. One of Gould's main complaints with authentic eighteenth-century harpsichords was the width of the keys, which are narrower than those of a traditional piano. This tended to throw off the amazing speed of his fingers. For that reason, there was only one kind of harpsichord in the world he could play: a Wittmayer. Made in Germany in the middle of the twentieth century, the Wittmayer harpsichord is five and a half feet in length, making it as big as a baby grand piano. Many harpsichord purists turned up their noses at Wittmayers, Gould knew, for precisely the reason he was so fond of them: Not only was the Wittmayer larger than most harpsichords, but the keyboard width is as close to a piano's as one could get. So he used a Wittmayer to record the first four Handel suites. Gould enjoyed himself immensely during the recording, but Edquist less so. A harpsichord is far more fragile than a piano and will go out of tune whenever the slightest breeze grazes it. Still worse, Gould had a tendency to hit the harpsichord's keys with the same force he used on a piano. As Edquist put it, Gould was "overzealous" in his attack. Not only was this unnecessary on a harpsichord (because the strings are plucked, you won't get a louder sound no matter how hard you hit the key), but it threw the keys out of position. Edquist spent hours on his knees in front of the instrument trying to undo the damage. "I just about cried like a baby," he said. "It's the closest I ever came to quitting."

When the recording came out, critics scratched their heads, wondering why the great Glenn Gould was suddenly recording on a harpsichord. Only a few people knew there was no deeper meaning to draw: that he was biding his time, waiting for his beloved instrument to return from New York.

In the meantime Gould continued to negotiate with Steinway & Sons over his proposal that trial pianos be shipped to Toronto. But it wasn't a particularly good time for him—or anyone else, for that matter—to ask for special dispensations from the company. Steinway & Sons had never recovered completely from the financial distress brought on by the Depression, then by the manufacturing restrictions during the war, then by a steady decline in piano sales around the country. Henry Z., for his part, had watched his father, Theodore, grow increasingly depressed by what had happened to the company forty years earlier and, ever the pragmatist, in 1972 he decided to sell the company to CBS. Suddenly Steinway & Sons became a very small subsidiary of a very large corporation. The change in ownership brought with it still more cost cutting.

The ripple effects were felt everywhere, including in Toronto.

After encountering a great deal of resistance from his contacts at Steinway, Gould all but gave up on the idea of getting them to send him pianos and found a Model D the CBC had on loan from Steinway that spent much of its time at Eaton's. Gould pronounced the piano "usable," but not much more.

Finally, more than a year after the piano's accident, Steinway & Sons phoned Muriel Mussen to say that CD 318 was repaired and ready to return to Toronto. When the piano arrived back at Eaton's, Edquist went straight over to examine it. He could tell that the case had been refurbished, the lid replaced, and everything else put back in its proper place and orientation. The keybed had been repaired, the key slip replaced. And he could tell there was a brand-new cast-iron plate inside.

That was the extent of the good news. Edquist noticed right away that only a few of the broken action parts had been replaced; the rest had merely been realigned, as if the Steinway workers were trying to save money on parts. He also noticed, after a quick tuning, that the tone was uneven and problematic in the treble. The higher notes were "all zingy and buzzy and didn't sound right." The treble, he discovered, had lost quite a bit of its timbre, depth, and singing quality.

The probable cause of the buzzing, Edquist decided, was the new plate. Every grand piano's action is custom-built around a cast-iron plate that has been uniquely fashioned for that particular piano. And each plate is a slightly different size. The difference is in millimeters, but those millimeters are crucial. The tiniest of differences in a plate's dimension and position are critical to how everything else fits together. Whenever an action is assembled, minute adjustments must be made to the mechanism's leverage and geometry as they relate to the plate. Edquist knew how important the plate is. Install a new plate in an old piano and you are inviting trouble: Issues with tone and touch are likely to arise, requiring modifications to the action. In 318's case, the few modifications that had been made to the action after the new plate was installed were insufficient at best.

Edquist called Franz Mohr in New York, whose response was
curt: "There's nothing I can do about it." So even before Gould
had a chance to sit down at the piano, Edquist wove some felt
into the small section of the strings between the tuning pins and
the metal bar known as the capo d'astro (this was a common
technique, but one 318 had never needed) to try to cut down on
the buzzing. It sounded better, but the unique timbre he had
come to associate with CD 318 was now largely attenuated.

When Gould sat down to the newly repaired piano, like a wine
expert sniffing a cork, he could tell right away that something was
off. Indeed, one of the first things Gould noticed was the "horrendous buzzing." But what his ears were hearing was quickly
eclipsed by what his hands were feeling. The action, he realized,
had taken a noticeable turn for the worse, with none of the responsiveness he had come to take for granted. Gould knew that
even after a thorough repair, CD 318 would not be the piano it had
been in 1969 and 1970—two especially productive years in the
recording studio—but he had hoped for an approximation. This
was no approximation. The piano was, for his purposes, an alien.

Rather than send it back, the two men decided to keep working on it in Toronto. Edquist did what he could—voicing and
revoicing, readjusting the blow distance on the hammers. But
Gould grew increasingly frustrated. The piano's action had lost
something essential, he decided, although he was unable to figure out exactly what it was. After a few weeks of what felt increasingly like pointless tinkering, Gould came up with a radical
idea: an action transplant. Could Edquist perhaps remove the
action from another Model D at Eaton's, which was seldom
played, and install it in CD 318? This, Gould reasoned, would
give Edquist a relatively clean slate of an action to work with
while preserving the fundamental magic of the rest of CD 318.

Edquist was immediately skeptical. The action of a piano slides out easily enough, and technicians routinely remove an action to work on it. But actions are not interchangeable. Every action is made to fit with the piano it resides in. "Glenn, it won't work," he complained. But Gould insisted, leaving Edquist with little choice but to make his point by demonstrating the difficulty of such an operation. "I knew I wasn't going to get out of there without trying it," he recalled. "When he wanted something, Glenn was one to push the needle in a millimeter at a time." So, with Gould pacing behind him, humming Bach, the tuner removed the actions from both pianos. He then put the other piano's action into 318, and indeed, as he predicted, he discovered that the hammers were so misaligned that they didn't even hit the strings in the right place. He showed the result to Gould, who was finally convinced and abandoned the plan.

In 1973, a year after CBS bought Steinway & Sons, the company further curtailed its largesse to Steinway artists by ending the practice of renting pianos for indefinite periods to its elite artists. The company began requiring that all Steinway artists buy their instruments.

Instead of bidding the piano a final farewell, on February 14, 1973, perhaps as a Valentine's Day gift to himself, Gould wrote a check to Steinway for $6,700 to purchase CD 318 outright. The invoice read, "1 Used, As Is, Steinway & Sons Model D Grand in Ebonized Case 317914." "Needless to say," Gould wrote to David Rubin at Steinway in a letter accompanying his check, "after all these years of exposure to the unique charms of CD 318, I am proud indeed to add it to my 'rare' instrument collection—and you may apply the adjective as you choose." In a nervous footnote, he asked almost timidly if the piano would retain its CD 318 designation. The answer, of course, was that it would not, because it was no longer the property of Steinway. The number

318 would be assigned to another concert piano in Steinway's stable.

Gould then asked Rubin for a formal reassurance that, now that the piano was in private hands, service on it would continue. He ended his letter in the most politic tone he could muster. "I want to thank you once again, and this time rather more officially than in the past, for your kindness and consideration this past year during which, for all intents and purposes, CD 318 was saved from the scrap-heap. I realize that the work of Franz and, undoubtedly, many other technicians at the factory as well, played a major role in the miraculous rebirth of the instrument, but I also realize that had it not been for your willingness to guide the project through the various experiments to which it was subjected, the final result would not have been the happy one which now makes it possible for us to record on this instrument once again."

He chose his words carefully, not wanting to jeopardize his relationship with Steinway now that he knew he would be relying on the company for future service. And he had no intention of letting on that he was in fact extremely frustrated by what had happened to CD 318. In buying the piano, Gould must have felt he had little choice. If Steinway had taken it back, who knows what might have happened. He was convinced that Steinway, famously unsentimental about its instruments, would not have spent the money to repair it a second time. He told Lorne Tulk he was afraid they would have simply destroyed it, "and he couldn't bear the thought of that," Tulk said.

Still, Tulk tried to talk Gould out of buying the piano, even resorting to an analogy to animals, a comparison he knew Gould could appreciate. "I said, 'It's like a horse or a dog that's served you very well, and it's time to put it out to pasture.'" Gould certainly understood, and perhaps even accepted Tulk's argument, but, as with the episode of the action transplant, he had trouble believing the piano couldn't be fixed. And, he reasoned to Tulk, there was nothing further he could do unless the piano belonged to him. "He bought it so he would have control over it," said Tulk years later, "so he could give it a dignified retirement." When Edquist heard Gould had bought 318, he was very surprised, as well as disappointed that Gould hadn't bothered to ask his opinion: "I would have advised him not to do it." At the same time, Edquist understood something fundamental about Gould: He was uniquely accustomed to having things go his way. He had grown up believing all traffic lights were green, even when they were red. And by purchasing 318, in spite of the botched repair attempts, he must have still held on to a shard of hope that the piano could be fixed.

What Tulk and others didn't know was that Gould was gradually losing control over another sacred part of his life. For more than a decade he had been in a serious, discreet romance with Cornelia Foss, the wife of the composer and conductor Lukas Foss.

Gould might have referred to himself as the Last Puritan, but that was probably more true about his approach to playing the piano than his sexuality. Gould grew up in a household where sex was not discussed, and throughout his life he maintained a discretion much like that of his parents, perhaps even more extreme. But he was hardly asexual. He had a tendency to develop adolescent crushes, and throughout his life he revered certain women from a distance. Once, when he was in his early twenties, he had a fairly lengthy relationship with a woman whose letters to him were addressed from "Faun" to "Spaniel." In fact, it was from "Faun" that he had taken over the rental of the Chickering before he purchased it.

But the most serious and long-lasting romantic relationship

of his life—it started when Gould was in his late twenties and
continued into his forties—was with Cornelia. It was also
perhaps the most emotionally turbulent of Gould's relationships, and triggered periods of absolute obsession for him.
Gould and Cornelia had met in 1959 by way of Gould's playing.
At the time, Lukas was teaching music at the University of California at Los Angeles, and one evening he and Cornelia were on
their way to a dinner party when a recording of the Goldberg
Variations came on the radio. Cornelia was at the wheel, and
Lukas insisted she pull over and stop the car in order to listen
without distraction. Lukas was entranced. Cornelia, who was
not a musician, was appreciative but not nearly as moved as her
husband was. She sat patiently while Lukas listened, spellbound,
to the entire thirty-eight minutes and twenty-six seconds of the
recording, which the radio station played without interruption.
When it was over, Lukas signaled Cornelia not to stir. "I have to
hear who this was." The announcer came on and identified the
performer as Glenn Gould. Oddly, in spite of the fame the
recording had brought Gould, it was the first time that Foss had
heard him.

But Foss, it turned out, was a musician whom Gould admired, and three years later, when playing in Los Angeles,
Gould invited the Fosses to the concert and the reception afterward. It was at the party that Gould first met Cornelia, a well-
regarded painter whose quick wit and breadth of knowledge
matched his own. The Fosses became close friends with Gould,
who took to calling them regularly. When Lukas became conductor of the Buffalo Symphony in 1963, Gould often drove
down from Toronto to visit. As the friendship progressed, the
conversations—and Gould's attention—began to shift focus.
When the three of them were together, Gould started out talking mostly to Lukas, then to the two of them, and before long
he was talking mostly to Cornelia. In the vibrant Cornelia he

had found his intellectual equal. One of Gould's gifts was his fugal mind: Not only was his ability to play counterpoint unmatched, but he could actually think on three or four levels at once. Having grown up around highly intelligent people, Cornelia was not the least bit intimidated. There were few subjects in which she was not conversant. In fact, Cornelia's worldliness contrasted sharply with Gould's relatively provincial upbringing. She had been born in Berlin, and when she was an infant her parents moved to Rome. When Cornelia was still a young girl, they fled Nazi Europe for the United States, where her father, Otto Brendel, a prominent archaeologist and art historian, taught first in Saint Louis and Indiana, then for many years at Columbia University. English was her third language.

In 1964 an affair began, and Cornelia and Gould met wherever they could: in New York, Buffalo, and Toronto. As the relationship grew more serious, Gould insisted that Cornelia move to Toronto and marry him. "He really didn't want this to be just an affair," she recalled many years later. After years of indecision, in 1968 Cornelia finally made up her mind to leave Lukas and move to Toronto. She put her son and daughter, ages ten and six, into the family station wagon along with the cat, and prepared to make a new life with Gould in Toronto. But Lukas, she recalled, wasn't so convinced of her resolve. While Cornelia sat in the car he stood in the driveway, smiling. "I said, 'Why are you smiling? I'm leaving you, for heaven's sake. I'm going to go off and marry Glenn,'" she recalled. "And he said, 'Don't be ridiculous, you're not going to marry Glenn. Have a good time. I'll see you next weekend.'"

Cornelia and Gould had decided more or less to live together but keep separate places. Cornelia enrolled her children in school in Toronto and rented a house a few blocks away from Gould's apartment, and they fell into something of a domestic routine. The couple even attended dinner parties given by

Gould's friends in the Toronto musical scene. For the most part, however, Gould kept this new turn in his life relatively quiet. Still, those who worked closely with him could not help but notice that something was different. Andrew Kazdin, for one, noted a newly domesticated tone to Gould's voice when he brought up Cornelia. "From time to time Glenn would bring her name up in conversations in a very matter-of-fact way, much the same as one would mention a marriage partner," Kazdin later wrote. Lorne Tulk described Cornelia as a "very, very lovely" woman. "Her mind was going all the time and his mind was going all the time, so the two of them got on very well," Tulk said. Gould seemed genuinely relaxed. And happy.

But there was a twist that Cornelia hadn't counted on. Within a few weeks of arriving in Toronto, Cornelia knew that her husband had been right: Marriage to Glenn Gould was out of the question. "I realized Glenn was an incredibly wonderful human being, the funniest, most wonderful person," she said. "But flawed. Something was seriously wrong." Not only did she now witness his myriad quirks on a daily basis, but she saw firsthand his growing dependence on prescription medication, mostly tranquilizers. Gould was not a person she could marry, and this fact became clear to her even before she had fully moved into her house. Yet it would take four and a half years to "disentangle" herself, as she later described it.

In those years, Cornelia lived something of a double life: Every Friday afternoon when school was out, she put the children in the station wagon, drove back to Buffalo, and spent the weekend with Lukas.

By 1973, the relationship between Gould and Cornelia was unraveling. Gould grew increasingly paranoid and insecure about her continued affection for him. He insisted on knowing her whereabouts at all times. If she had an appointment, he drove her there and waited in the car for one, two, three hours—however long it lasted. In a way she found it touching. "He was passionate about everything he did," she would say years later. But his obsessive devotion to her was now giving way to paranoia. And it revealed a side of him that few people saw at close range.

Cornelia attributed some of Gould's paranoid behavior to the large amounts of medication he was taking, a regimen that by the early 1970s included ten Valiums a day. Eventually the relationship had become stifling for her, and she began to plan her exit from Toronto and a return to Lukas, who was now living in New York City. She and Lukas decided that he should drive to Toronto to get the children, by then aged ten and fourteen, and take them first, without telling Glenn. Cornelia knew that as soon as Gould discovered that the children were gone he would be beside himself, because he would understand what it meant: that she, too, was leaving. Indeed, when he found out that Lukas had come for the children, he was furious. She stated plainly that she would be leaving soon. And she did.

Gould had always avoided braiding his public and private lives, and for weeks leading up to the separation, and even afterward, those he worked with had no notion that anything was amiss. "It was not well defined exactly when her name began to fade from his conversations," wrote Kazdin. "I just sort of sat up one day and realized that he had ceased speaking of her. She was never mentioned again." But when Cornelia left, privately Gould was devastated. He called her in New York and insisted on staying on the phone for hours at a time. When she told him he needed to get some exercise and fresh air, perhaps take a walk around the block, he agreed, but insisted that she stay on the phone while he went out. When he put the phone down, she picked up a book and read until he returned. This telephonic struggle went on for more than a year, at which point Gould announced that he planned to visit Cornelia in New

York. His goal was to persuade her to return to Toronto. By now it was summertime and she was renting a small cottage on Long Island. Gould arrived and checked into a nearby motel, and they took a walk on the beach in the June heat. Years later Cornelia could still remember others on the beach in their bathing suits, staring at the figure next to her in his heavy coat and gloves. She told him she could not return to Toronto, and said good-bye to him at the motel. They made a date to talk on the phone in a week's time. Then Cornelia did the unthinkable: She forgot to call. When she remembered, and when he finally took her call, he told her he now knew she no longer loved him. Still, they talked, and made a date for her to call again. But again she forgot. And that was the end. They never spoke again.

CORNELIA WAS AN obsession Gould couldn't shake. Rather than read her neglect as a sign of evident rejection and adjust accordingly, Gould continued to fixate. Discovered among his private papers after his death was a handwritten page dating to 1976, chronicling frequent attempts to reach someone, presumably Cornelia, made over a period of several days. The page paints a portrait of near-desperate attempts to speak with Cornelia. She was apparently being shielded by other family members, including Lukas and her daughter. The entry ended after the third day of unreturned phone calls: "Called at 11:35. L. said he would 'try to get you to call.'" After that, Gould evidently abandoned his efforts to reach her. Not long after, still obsessing, he filled another four pages with a list of "pros" and "cons," reviewing the state of the relationship. He was careful not to specify that he was referring to his broken relationship with Cornelia and kept the tone distant and clinical. Reasons to "retain" the relationship included: "because I feel, at this moment, that the daily or stand-by contact with one individual is essential" and "because I cannot easily surrender the tokens of permanence—safety, security, shelter—from my overview of life." Why he "would like to be without it" included: "because it involves an unmanageable breakdown in communications, a constant frustration which leads to the avoidance of all that discussion which once made it meaningful" and "because I feel that the long, long history of quarrels and relationship disruptions is bound to be continued indefinitely and that that continuance will be detrimental to my health—physical as well as emotional." Gould then composed a third lengthy section under the heading WHAT WOULD I ADVISE IN THE ROLE OF 3RD-PARTY OBSERVER. Included in that column was "immediate discontinuance," and "that I, as observed party, would adjust given time to a new set of proportions in my life and, eventually, would wonder what ever made it seem like an addicting habit."

Reading Gould's clinical pros-and-cons discussion is striking for various reasons, not the least of which being that it contradicts the popular notion of Gould as a hermit. Hermits, of course, aren't known for their need for "daily contact" with another person. But more remarkable is the fact that although Cornelia had essentially ended the relationship three years earlier, Gould continued to believe that he was in control of steering its future course.

It was the same impulse—or fantasy—that guided his belief that he could salvage his piano. And now he had all the more reason to resurrect the instrument. Some years earlier Gould had begun a collaboration with Bruno Monsaingeon, a French violinist and filmmaker. Their work together yielded two series of films celebrating the genius that was Glenn Gould. One was called *Music and Terminology (Chemins de la Musique)*. The other was a series of three films titled *Glenn Gould Plays Bach*. The projects spanned several years, and for most of those years 318 was the piano he used. It appeared in the films with its right side banged and dented, but its sound was still rich and splendid.

When the filming began in 1974, Monsaingeon found CD 318 to be a perfectly fine instrument. He remembers that for the tremendous range of repertoire Gould was playing in the first set of films—Bach, Scriabin, Schoenberg, Gibbons, Wagner, and the Berg sonata—the piano was "magnificent," producing not only a full-blooded sound but a Baroque one as well. "It was a piano with that kind of range," he said.

As he did during the recording sessions, during the filming Edquist stood by most of the time, and whenever the slightest problem arose, Gould would stop and call him over to regulate the piano. Then, Monsaingeon recalled, Edquist, "that modest, peaceful man, would step up and start working on it." Tulk was in the films too, displaying his mastery of tape splicing and mixing during a mock recording session—made specifically for the film—in Eaton Auditorium. Evident, too, was Gould's love of being in the studio, in close contact with the dials, switches, and levers, all in the name of perfecting a performance with technology. More than once he seized control of the mixing board to get just the level he wanted on each track, to the patient amusement of Tulk and everyone else.

Yet Gould continued to brood about the state CD 318 was in. He noted that the tempos in his first recordings on the restored piano, and now in the films, were slower than he would have liked. The action he so loved was suddenly holding him back. Perhaps thinking that Edquist wasn't doing all he could for the piano, in a fit of infidelity Gould asked Steinway to have Franz Mohr fly up and work on the piano. Now, however, all repairs would be done at Gould's expense, since he, not Steinway, owned the piano. Mohr arrived and did some adjusting to the capstan screws, raising the level of the hammers. (Edquist grumbled afterward that these were all things he could have done, thus saving Mohr a trip and Gould some money.) Mohr left Toronto shaking his head. Although he was accustomed to pianos in various states of disrepair, this one was a mess. It was just plain old and simply worn out. Although Mohr had spent many years indulging pianists in their loyalty to—even obsession with—their instruments, in the end he was a believer in the Steinway credo that the company was in the business of selling and promoting new pianos, not endlessly restoring the old instruments with their brittle wood and fading sound.

But Gould wasn't giving up.

In early 1976, he decided to send the piano to Steinway for a second attempt at repair. This time he circumvented the usual bureaucracy and called Mohr directly. Mohr had spent enough time working on CD 318 to know exactly what the piano needed: the careful and precise measurement of each key's weight in order to restore its evenness of touch. Mohr was expert at this. When he had rebuilt Horowitz's piano he did so painstakingly, key by key. To ensure precision, Mohr had created a chart of all the parts, listing the gram weight of each key. As he rebuilt the piano, he duplicated the weight and action as precisely as possible. This was what needed to happen with CD 318.

But Mohr was too busy to oversee the work directly. Horowitz was in one of his productive periods, and Mohr's near-slavish devotion to the artist, who was now seventy-six, left him little time to attend to the eccentric Canadian. The best he could do was give precise instructions to Joe Bisceglie, the long-time employee who now presided over the factory. Mohr gave Gould his word that he would do his very best to convey exactly what the pianist wanted: an action with keys weighted uniformly down to the milligram to give the keyboard a light, even, hair-trigger touch.

Mohr also spoke with Bill Hupfer, the man whom Gould had accused years earlier of delivering the crippling blow to his shoulder. Mohr told Hupfer about Gould's requirements, especially the need for a light, even touch. "I told Bill he didn't want a romantic Steinway," Mohr recalled. But Hupfer, not surprisingly, wasn't about to drop everything to oversee the rebuilding of Glenn Gould's quirky and by now very elderly piano. The conversation made it clear to Mohr that no one in the upper echelons of the company planned to give the piano special attention.

A few weeks after the piano arrived back in Astoria, technicians at the factory came up with an official recommendation for what should be done to the piano, which the company now referred to as "formerly CD 318": install new backchecks with stiffer wire, reregulate or replace repetition springs, and reweigh the action "to obtain a uniform down-weight." This last item, it was noted, was critical. The outlook was promising.

DURING THE PIANO's absence, Gould tried several of the newer instruments at Eaton's. Throughout the 1960s, when 318 was in good working order, Gould had been largely unaffected by the fact that during those years the quality of Steinway pianos was suffering badly. Every once in a while the factory would get it right, but usually the pianos being produced were just plain inferior to the company's prewar instruments. Steinway was putting excessive amounts of lead in its keys, which made it easier to depress a key, but the extra mass created a kind of inertia or sluggishness in the action, which most pianists disliked. In 1963, in an effort to overcome problems it was having with its actions, Steinway started replacing all the cloth bushings with Teflon. It was a disaster, because although the Teflon did not alter in size as a result of changes in humidity, the wood surrounding it did. This made for actions that were too tight in the humid summer months and too loose in the winter. The result was an inconsistent level of friction in the action's parts, as well as an annoying clicking noise that pianists could hear.

More and more frequently, concert grands were showing signs of bad craftsmanship. During one recital, the Brazilian pianist Ney Salgado was in the middle of Ravel's difficult *Alborado del Gracioso* when several keys simply stopped working. Another artist, Byron Janis, was playing Rachmaninoff's Piano Concerto in G Minor when one of the ebony keys flew right off the piano. Suddenly a tiny jagged piece of wood jabbed his finger where the B-flat had been a second before.

This period was especially hard on touring pianists. By the early 1970s, costs had risen to the point where few musicians could afford to tour with their own personal pianos. It could cost up to a thousand dollars to ship a piano from New York to Chicago. Veteran concert performer Gary Graffman came up with his own extreme solution. Before going on tour he consulted his Truth Box, a card file indexed by city and state, with his personal appraisal of the pianos available in each place. If the card indicated the piano was a dud, Graffman complained bitterly to Steinway until a suitable instrument was provided. When Ruth Laredo encountered a lousy piano or a restless audience, it could intensify her nervousness. Less frequently, when she found a piano in a strange city that was fine, her playing wasn't merely more relaxed: She found herself inspired. Laredo learned to be philosophical about bad pianos, which enhanced her appreciation of good ones. "Actually, I think all the bad instruments improved my playing," she once said.

Some pianists were more amenable than others to playing on alien instruments. For Arthur Rubinstein, "Every piano is a different adventure." And there was the Russian pianist Sviatoslav Richter, who believed one simply had to have faith in the piano and trust in the tuner who had worked on it. For this reason, Richter never tried a piano before going onstage, preferring instead to take each piano he encountered as a sign of destiny. Monsaingeon, who made a lengthy film about Richter, recalled the pianist saying, "You've just got to believe, like a disciple of Christ believing Christ could walk on water, and if you don't believe it, he will drown."

Although Gould no longer had to contend with the vagaries of catch-as-catch-can pianos, the ripple effects of Steinway's decline in quality were evident to him as well. Someone recorded one of Gould's several forays to Eaton's, where he did brief ad hoc performances while trying out several of their newer instruments and offered a running critique of the modern Steinway. On CD 131, "otherwise known as the Mussen special" (presumably because it was a piano Muriel Mussen had foisted on a great many visiting performers), he played a little Bach and some Strauss and pronounced the piano's action "very sluggish," even "heavy and cumbersome." And, warming to his material: "But it's also very even, so it's evenly sluggish." The piano, he went on to complain, lost its tuning very quickly. "It has even gone out of tune the two minutes I've been playing on it."

Gould may have been trying different pianos at Eaton's and elsewhere in Toronto, but in the meantime the work down in Astoria was going according to plan—but not Gould's plan. "To my dismay," Mohr wrote years later in his memoir, "when I went to the factory and put my fingers on the piano, I knew that Gould would not be pleased." The action was much too heavy. The technicians had made it into the type of big romantic instrument that many pianists liked but that Gould abhorred. Mohr knew he could revoice the former CD 318. But he also knew that the sound was not what would upset Gould. It was the touch. And that was something that simply could not be restored.

This time, rather than have the piano shipped home, Gould

went to New York to try it out. As Mohr tells the story, Gould arrived, put his hands on the rebuilt 318, and nearly broke into tears. " 'This is not my piano,' he moaned. 'What has happened to this piano? I cannot play it; I cannot use it.' " In his memoir Mohr observed that "the poor man was completely lost." It was five years since the piano had been dropped, and the repeated attempts at repair had all been in vain. Gould returned home in a somber mood.

Once again the instrument was shipped back to Toronto. The soul, if not the body, that was CD 318 had been left somewhere on the factory floor in Astoria. Or was it beneath the loading dock, where it landed after having been dropped? Whatever, wherever, one thing was clear: The magic that might have eluded others but that Glenn Gould revered was gone forever.

Oddly, for all his anguish Gould continued to record on CD 318. He decided that although the escalating problems made performing difficult for him as a pianist, they were subtle enough not to be heard in the final taping. And it wasn't that he found the piano unplayable; he just found it increasingly difficult to get what he wanted from it. He recorded Bach's English Suites and a number of Mozart sonatas, and he continued filming with Bruno Monsaingeon. Yet by the late 1970s, the topic of the instrument's diminished quality began to come up during the filming sessions, and the filmmaker also noticed. "It had deteriorated very drastically," he said. "I quite agreed that there was something dead in the sound of the piano. It had become an uneven piano, a non-pianistic piano."

Then Gould started canceling the filming sessions.

AT THE TIME, Gould was keeping a diary that chronicled a terrible problem he believed he was having with his hands. The journal reveals a man in the midst of a full-blown crisis, similar to

the aftermath of the paralyzing blow Bill Hupfer had allegedly
inflicted nearly two decades earlier. But this time Gould kept
everything to himself.

Although Gould's hands were unusually well suited to the
piano—his fingers were flexible, long, and strong—he was
perennially anxious about them. He protected, coddled, and
soaked them, dipped them in melted wax, and continually fret-
ted over them. In the late 1970s he filled page after page of
yellow-lined notepads with minute details of what he came to
view as a serious and potentially crippling problem at the keyboard. It started with a "lack of coordination" that he first noticed in June 1977. What he had always taken for granted—the
naturalness and ease of his piano technique—had been lost. He
began a series of "practice experiments," spending several hours
at a time playing repertoire "constants" like Bach toccatas and
Haydn sonatas, trying to remedy the problem. He analyzed in
agonizing detail every aspect of his playing: not just his hands
but his posture, and the position of his arms, elbows, wrists,
neck, head, and chest. He shifted his body's center of gravity; he
experimented with the curvature of his spine.

The experience was unnerving. Gould had always maintained a simple faith in his musical gifts. He often refused, when
asked, to expound on the mechanics of what he did because
playing the piano had always come to him so naturally. "I don't
want to think too much about my playing or I'll get like that
centipede who was asked which foot he moved first and became
paralyzed just thinking about it," he said to an interviewer early
in his career. But now the ease with which his hands moved
seemed to have disappeared. His head and his hands had gone
completely "out of sync," he wrote.

It was a difficult time, to be sure. The end of the relationship
with Cornelia had come just two years after the death of his
mother, Florence, in 1975, which one friend called "probably the

most traumatic event" of Gould's life. And he was likely suffering a variety of side effects from the excessive amount of medication he was taking for his many ailments. He had developed hypertension, and although his regular doctor had told him not to give it a second thought, Gould consulted a second physician who prescribed an anti-hypertensive drug. Now checking and recording his blood pressure every hour—and sometimes every fifteen minutes—Gould added the hypertension medication to a regimen that included an antispasmodic for cramping in his stomach, anti-inflammatory medication for his shoulder discomfort, and a steady diet of tranquilizers. In addition to these miseries, Gould also had overly sensitive teeth and experienced pain when urinating.

Friends and acquaintances began to notice that he looked haggard. Soon after Gould started obsessing about his hands, Peter Ostwald, an old acquaintance, visited him in Toronto and was "shocked" by the deterioration in his appearance since he had last seen him a decade earlier. "His face and body had become bloated. He looked fat, flabby, and stooped," Ostwald later wrote in a book about Gould. Ostwald, a psychiatrist, noted that the anti-hypertensive might have caused the weight gain, but observed that Gould's "skin, which had always been on the pale side, had acquired an unnatural grayness."

Gould's obsession with his hands may have had something to do with his escalating battle with Steinway & Sons over CD 318. The damage—or what he perceived as damage—done at the Steinway factory had been a big blow, and he was deeply worried about what to do next. Although it's not clear if Gould ever made the connection himself, it is entirely possible that at least part of the problem with his hands lay in the rebuilt action of 318, which had returned from its latest trip to New York with too much lead in the keys. For a pianist like Gould, who placed such strict demands on himself for speed and precision, playing on a sluggish, improperly balanced action could well have caused him to think there was something wrong with his own fingers.

Another cause of stress was the temporary loss of his favorite recording studio, which occurred when Eaton Auditorium was closed for renovations. For the entirety of 1978 Gould did no recording at all. Instead he spent a great deal of time writing detailed accounts of his hand condition, as well as other ailments. In May 1979, Gould and his team were informed by Eaton's that the renovation of the auditorium had stalled, and although the place was a mess, if they thought they could make usable recordings there, they were welcome to try. As quickly as they had appeared, Gould's hand symptoms suddenly vanished, and he was ready to resume recording.

In fact, as Kazdin later recalled, Eaton Auditorium looked as though a bomb had hit the place. Walls were missing. Doors were boarded up. There were no lights and no heat. Still worse, water tanks on the roof had burst and the whole auditorium had flooded. As a result, the flooring had been ripped up and in its place was a carpet of ceiling plaster that had fallen from the floor above. Thick layers of dust covered everything.

Nevertheless Gould decided to tough it out in the construction zone. Ray Roberts and his son spent days cleaning it up, and, in an effort to bring the room up to a temperature Gould could live with, they brought in large propane heaters and used portable desk and floor lamps for lighting. Fortunately, the freight elevator still functioned, so the piano could be moved in and out. When it was brought in, Edquist would work to get it in tune, but as soon as the temperature fluctuated more than a few degrees, it fell out of tune again.

When Gould got back to recording and filming, there was absolutely no sign of any deterioration in his playing. Not only had he overcome the whole hand crisis, but it was as if nothing had happened. Still, he was less and less happy with the piano that CD 318 had become. In recording sessions, Gould and Edquist and Roberts tried any number of gambits to make it sound better. They positioned it differently on the stage. They changed the location of the microphones, backing them away from the piano as if it were an aging actress in need of soft lighting. Finally, in the course of one frustrating recording session, Edquist said to Gould, by way of a joke, "Glenn, maybe you should try a Yamaha." Although Edquist was not seriously urging Gould to abandon Steinway in favor of a mass-produced Japanese import, both men knew that, short of a miracle, 318 was not to be revived.

IN THE SUMMER of 1980, Gould decided to bet his hand on a miracle. He was scheduled to visit New York that June for a photo session with Don Hunstein, the well-known photographer of musical celebrities. (The *Freewheelin' Bob Dylan* album cover is one of his hallmark shots.)

Gould had Edquist take 318's action out of the piano and persuaded Ray Roberts to drive with him down to New York to deliver the action to Steinway & Sons for yet another attempt at resuscitation. Roberts wedged the five-foot-long mechanism into the back of Longfellow, Gould's large Lincoln Town Car, and they set off on the five-hundred-mile trip to New York City.

Gould was on edge about the trip well before it began. He started a lengthy diary entry on June 13, 1980 ("And it's Friday, too!!"). Roberts had been suffering from a cold, so Gould insisted that he stay out of the car for at least thirty-six hours before they left.

Gould, who was a notoriously bad driver, insisted on taking the wheel. Roberts can't have relished this situation, since Gould's reputation was well earned—and one that the maestro acknowledged freely and with good humor. "I suppose it can be said that I'm an absent-minded driver," he once said. "It's true that I've driven through a number of red lights on occasion, but on the other hand I've stopped at a lot of green ones but never gotten credit for it."

Gould's fretting began the moment the two men started packing up the car. A lengthy discussion ensued about whether they should wrap the action in some kind of padding, but they decided against it, reasoning that any jouncing would just stimulate the natural movement of the hammers anyway. Besides, Gould worried, once they reached the border, anything shrouded might arouse the curiosity of the customs inspectors. In fact Edquist had made several initial inquiries with customs officials about the traveling piano action, in order to ease its passage across the border, and had composed a letter explaining why it needed to be transported to America. It was addressed "To Whom it May Concern":

> Only the manufacturer has the capability of rebuilding this mechanism to factory specifications. Due to the very critical nature of the artist's usage of the piano, it is imperative that this work be undertaken by Steinway factory technicians where the piano was manufactured, using Steinway replacement parts. There is no Steinway repair shop in Canada having this expertise.

Stranger things have shown up at the Canadian-U.S. border, to be sure, but the sight of Glenn Gould in the summertime warmth, wrapped in his scarf, gloves, and heavy coat, could hardly have gone unnoticed. Add to that the guts of his piano splayed on the backseat of his enormous car, and the two travelers were certain to raise eyebrows.

The two men had left Toronto late in the evening, so by the

time they reached the border just north of Buffalo at Niagara Falls, it was nearly three A.M. When the U.S. customs inspectors looked in the car, Roberts took charge. He got out of the car and showed them Edquist's brief letter, stating that the cargo in question was the mechanism of Steinway Grand Piano #318, then invited the inspectors to take a closer look. He explained that it was a part of a piano that was going to the States for repair and then returning, and therefore not something on which they would need to collect a duty. He cocked his head in the direction of Gould, who was at the wheel. "Show-biz guy," he said conspiratorially. They were waved through.

The two men left the action in the car and spent the night at a Holiday Inn in Batavia, New York, 350 miles from New York City. The following morning they continued on to another Holiday Inn just outside New York City, a hotel Gould patronized regularly. But Gould was unhappy about the air-conditioning there, so in a classic move for the exquisitely sensitive Gould, he drove into New York and took a room at the Drake Hotel on Fifth Avenue, another regular haunt. But, finding the mattresses too hard and the entire place reeking of fresh paint, Gould insisted on driving back to the Holiday Inn. The action made the trip as well, strapped all the while in the backseat of the car. The men were functioning on almost no sleep by this point, and the next day they drove back into New York ("I navigated in New York like an acerbic cabbie," he wrote) and dropped the action off at Steinway.

Having done so, Gould and Roberts drove to the recording studio on Thirtieth Street, where Gould was to meet Hunstein for the shoot. While there, Gould spent a long time playing CD 41, a piano favored by Horowitz. He liked the piano's full-bodied sound but found the action erratic. "Furthermore, it buzzes as indeed does 201 to a lesser extent," he wrote, referring to one of

Rachmaninoff's favorite pianos, which had a "terrific action," but no real high notes and a dull, worn-out bass. "It's as though some rare disease was sweeping the Steinway species or, alternately, that my hearing is suddenly aware of a level of sensitivity which was never bothersome before." Gould explained to the ever-patient Mohr that he needed "the sound of the one and the action of the other."

Later that day, he went to the Steinway Basement "to see what's around." His disappointment deepened. "All were miserable, undistinguished," he lamented to his diary. Even CD 82, a new piano that Franz Mohr had assured him would not disappoint, buzzed terribly. The entire situation, he decided, was tragic and disgusting. He could not wait to leave. "For me," he later wrote, "Manhattan is still one of the most depressing places on earth."

Returning to the Holiday Inn that evening, the dejected Gould called his friend Robert Silverman, the publisher of the *Piano Quarterly*, who had good contacts at a number of piano manufacturers, and asked him about local dealers for Hamburg Steinways, which, most pianists now agreed, were superior to the models made in America, especially when it came to touch. Silverman told Gould he would talk to the Hamburg Steinway dealer, but urged him not to abandon the American Steinway just yet.

The next day Gould called Franz Mohr. "I told him of my severe disillusionment with 41 and with the pianos in the Basement," he later wrote. "He said that, if I was bothered by buzzing in a new inst like 82, there was little point in changing hammers on 318 and (doing a 180 degree turn) that I should send the chassis to the Factory and have them determine whether anything could be loose inside." Send the chassis to New York to see if something was loose? What were they going to do? Hold it upside down and shake it? Mohr clearly had other priorities, and Gould was losing patience with the senior concert specialist. "I have finally lost all confidence in Franz," he wrote. "His inability to fathom the tonal and action mechanical inadequacy of 41 and of the other beasts in the Basement, his inability to hear (or to admit to hearing) the buzz syndrome, his inability to act succinctly on behalf of 318 are hardly encouraging." Gould returned to Canada, in more doubt than ever before about the future of his long association with Steinway & Sons.

TEN

The Defection

In 1981 Gould rerecorded the Goldberg Variations, and the album was released the following year, a few weeks before his death in October 1982. Photograph by Don Hunstein, courtesy of Sony BMG Music Entertainment.

CD 318's CROWNING INDIGNITY came in 1980, quite literally in the middle of Bach's *Well-Tempered Clavier*. Gould and Monsaingeon were making one of their final films together—the second in a series called *Glenn Gould Plays Bach*, in which Gould played the Fugue in E Major from Book II. Halfway into the piece, Gould simply stopped playing. The action was not the problem. It was the sound. Where the piano had once been rich and supple in tone, it was now feeble and weak, barely projecting. Gradually he and Monsaingeon came to accept that he couldn't finish the piece on the venerable 318. So in the middle of the recording they substituted a different piano, while maintaining the illusion in the film that he was playing on a single instrument.

A few months later, Gould summoned Edquist to Eaton Auditorium, which was still in a shambles after the flood and renovations. Gould was there to record a Bach prelude and fugue. To Edquist's immense surprise, Gould had taken seriously his offhand remark about trying a Japanese import. There, in the old recording space, sat Gould before a nine-foot Yamaha.

Edquist wasn't impressed, to say the least. For one thing, the piano was noisy. When Gould released the sustaining pedal slowly, the dampers would zip into the strings, creating an annoying buzz. Edquist spent hours needling the dampers in an effort to mitigate the noise. And he fine-tuned it for what seemed like hours. But in the end he found the entire exercise of working on the Yamaha frustrating and pointless, and found himself pining for the original 318, as stable an instrument as he had ever known.

Gould was by now finally ready to accept the fact that the intense, exclusive intimacy of a life with one piano—*the* piano—

had finally ended. But he had no patience left for the long, frustrating spells of substitute pianos while 318 was being worked on in New York. He called his friend Robert Silverman to help him find another piano—not a temporary substitute, but a permanent replacement. Gould had recently made a major decision to rerecord the Goldberg Variations, more than twenty-five years after his first recording had made him an overnight sensation.

There were various reasons for his decision, beginning with technology. The 1955 version existed only in mono sound, and the development of stereo, digital, and Dolby all fascinated Gould. Over the years he had experimented in studios, both at Eaton and in New York, with these newly developed audio technologies, and now he wanted to rerecord the piece that had launched his career with the benefit of everything the state-of-the-art studio had to offer.

And there were musical reasons as well: Gould had something new to say about the piece. He wanted to record a cohesive interpretation that could act as a corrective to what he considered the scattered performance of twenty-five years earlier, which he now found buoyant but altogether too romantic, too "pianistic" in the worst sense of the word. For a long time he had been saying he planned to wrap up his performing career at around the time he turned fifty. Taking on the piece that launched his fame clearly represented a meaningful ending. Another consideration may have been a lingering insecurity about his technique after the protracted episode with his hands. What better way to reassure himself—and show the world—than, on the eve of turning fifty, to nail the piece that made him famous at age twenty-two?

But first he needed a piano on which to accomplish this feat.

Thus began a series of phone calls to New York. Though fully aware of the long and now-famous rift between Gould and

Steinway, Silverman's first call was to the Steinway headquarters on Fifty-seventh Street, inquiring what they might have available. Bruce Stevens, the president, called back with three possibilities: two Model D concert grands in Manhattan, and one in the showroom in Long Island City.

Silverman hung up the phone and called Baldwin, knowing full well that at this point the situation was turning sensitive. Signing on as a Steinway artist was tantamount to taking a loyalty oath. Even casually playing an instrument of a different make was considered a breach of trust that could threaten a pianist's standing as a Steinway artist. But actively seeking another make of piano for purposes of performing or recording while under contract to Steinway was considered a breach of contract as well as a major betrayal. So when Silverman called Jack Romann, the artistic manager of Baldwin, he asked for discretion. He explained to Romann that Glenn Gould was looking for a new piano and asked if there was a Baldwin he could look at, or perhaps a Bechstein. (Baldwin was representing Bechstein in the U.S. at the time.) To snatch a major musician like Gould away from Steinway would have been a huge coup for Baldwin, whose concert grands, once considered on a par with Steinway and Bösendorfer, had been all but forgotten by 1980. But while competitive, Romann was also honest, and he was sufficiently familiar with what he euphemistically referred to as "Gould's technical requirements" to know what to say. He told Silverman that he did not have a single decent piano for Mr. Gould to try.

When Franz Mohr heard that Gould was looking for a piano on which to record the Goldberg Variations again, he of course knew precisely which instrument would be ideal: Horowitz's main studio piano, known as CD 186, which was locked up in a corner of the Steinway Basement. Mohr knew the instrument had the uniformly light touch that Gould adored, and Mohr himself had attended to CD 186 constantly and lovingly for more than a decade. Mohr knew Gould's pianistic needs well enough to know that this was the best piano in town for the task, and for a brief moment he considered asking Horowitz if he might lend the piano to Gould for the recording. But in the end he didn't dare approach the mercurial Horowitz, who had never been warmly inclined toward his Canadian rival, about letting Gould borrow the instrument. So Mohr let the matter drop rather than create problems for himself.

Unwittingly, Mohr had created a big problem for Steinway. A few weeks later, Silverman called Gould with some news. He had spoken with someone at the Ostrovsky Piano and Organ Company, the Yamaha dealer in New York, and the store had pianos for him to try. Gould asked Ray Roberts to contact Ostrovsky to set up a visit, and after a few calls Roberts was connected to Raphael Mostel, the only salesman in the shop that day who also happened to be a musician. The first thing Roberts asked was whether the store had any nine-foot grands. Mostel responded that there were two, and asked his own question: Who was the prospective buyer? Roberts explained that this was an especially delicate topic, because the pianist in question, one of international renown, had been under contract to Steinway for nearly twenty-five years, and if Steinway were to learn that this pianist was even thinking of a different brand, the consequences could be bitterly unpleasant. Therefore, if the pianist were to come into the store to try the pianos, it would have to be after hours, and the store would have to take measures to ensure that no one could see anything from the outside. To Mostel, the insistence on such secretiveness was understandable but also a little extreme. "There was a very cloak-and-dagger tone to the conversation," he said, "almost as if there were true peril involved."

Mostel agreed to the excessive precautions, but insisted that if he were to go to all this trouble, he would need to know who the pianist was. Roberts relented and told him it was none other than Glenn Gould. Like everyone in the music business and even the public at large, Mostel knew that Gould had become increasingly reclusive over the years, cultivating an aura of Howard Hughes–like secrecy. He was heard only on his recordings and seen in public only occasionally on Canadian television. Of course Mostel instantly agreed to the conditions. "I said, 'Whatever he needs, as long as I can be in the room when he plays.'" After all, it had been nearly two decades since Gould had given up the concert stage. They arranged for Gould to come into Ostrovsky's after six o'clock, when the store closed.

Gould had not been to New York since the ill-fated trip with the action a year earlier. This time, without the added worry of having CD 318's action on the backseat, the trip across the border went much more smoothly, and Gould and Roberts proceeded directly to the Drake Hotel. First, to appease both Silverman and Steinway, Gould went to the Steinway Basement to try the two pianos that Bruce Stevens had recommended.

He hated them.

He even went to Long Island City to try a piano there. First he loved it, and for an incredible twenty-four hours it seemed as if the problem had been solved and all would be well between the demanding pianist and his long-suffering sponsor. "He called and said he had found it, and that he would go back in the morning and try it again," Silverman said. But by the next day, the infatuation had evaporated. When he called Silverman the next morning, this time from Long Island City, he said, simply, "It's not the piano."

Later that day, Gould and Roberts went to Ostrovsky's piano showroom, which was located, along with half a dozen other piano dealers, on the block between Broadway and Seventh Avenue on West Fifty-sixth Street, just a few hundred feet from Carnegie Hall.

Boris Ostrovsky, a prominent piano technician, had been selling pianos in the U.S. for years and was the exclusive Yamaha dealer in the greater New York area during the 1960s and 1970s, when the Japanese piano manufacturer was establishing a solid presence in North America. It was the same period that Steinway found itself struggling against a recurring threat from a handful of Steinway artists who were frequently, and vocally, expressing their disappointment in Steinway's pianos—and threatening to abandon Steinway for Yamaha. Unlike Steinway, Yamaha had avoided establishing an artist policy, but the company went out of its way to cultivate pianists whose affections for Steinway were waning. If Yamaha did manage to lure one away from Steinway, it assigned a full-time technician to the musician to service and tune his instrument.

Boris Ostrovsky made a point of keeping two or three well-maintained concert grands in his showroom. When he died in the 1970s, his wife, Debbi, took over the business. Debbi Ostrovsky was not a pianist or a piano technician; nor, before her husband's death, was she much of a businesswoman. And she certainly wasn't enthusiastic about keeping the store open late and covering the windows so that Glenn Gould could come in and play her pianos in absolute privacy. But at Mostel's urging she relented. There were two nine-foot concert grands in the store at the time, one brand-new one that had just arrived and another that had been broken in: a five-year-old piano that the store's head technician once referred to as "Mitsuo's baby." The piano had undergone careful regulating by Ostrovsky's most skilled technician, a Japanese tuner named Mitsuo Azuma, who had spent hundreds of hours working obsessively on the instrument in his spare time.

The demand for discretion and privacy presented a particular challenge to the showroom, which had been built out of three connecting carriage houses that shared a huge expanse of floor-to-ceiling windows with no curtains, shades, or any other means of covering the sea of glass that fronted onto Fifty-sixth Street. Azuma's piano was not just in the front of the third store; it was squarely in the window. So Mostel arrived at work the day of the Gould appointment with a suitcase filled with sheets he had brought from home and, that evening after the store closed, he taped them across the windows of the first and third showrooms.

The only store employees who were present when Gould and Roberts arrived were Mostel, Ostrovsky, and her secretary. After a generous exchange of pleasantries, Mostel showed Gould both pianos and suggested that he would probably prefer the older piano to the new one. From a standing position, Gould struck a few notes on the newer piano and immediately lost interest. He then walked over to the piano in the window, hit a few notes, sat down, and began playing. First he played a few things to try out the different registers, then he launched into Bach. He nodded to Roberts, who immediately—and to everyone else present, mysteriously—left the room. Gould appeared delighted. "This is the best-regulated piano I've ever played," he told Debbi Ostrovsky. After a few minutes Roberts reappeared with the old pygmy chair, whose seat now consisted of nothing more than a wooden crossbar upon which Gould perched.

Even before announcing that he planned to buy the piano, Gould asked Ostrovsky about the technician who had worked on it. This question put her in a bind, because even before it was apparent that Mitsuo Azuma had done the impossible—taking a standard Yamaha concert grand and turning it into an amazing instrument that would suit the needs of the great Glenn Gould—she had known that he was a uniquely talented technician. But she wasn't about to lose a staff technician to Glenn Gould. So instead of answering the question, she dithered and assured Gould that she would find him an excellent technician.

After ten minutes or so the two women left the room, leaving Mostel alone with the pianist. Gould kept playing. Mostel's reward for his efforts was what amounted to a private concert from one of the finest musicians in the world. The fact that the live performance was from someone who had long since forsworn playing in public made it all the more thrilling. "The whole experience of seeing him play was peculiar. His nose was at the keyboard, and he was completely lost in the playing," Mostel recalled. "When one hand stopped playing it was conducting the other. He was arguing with himself, physically. It seemed to be a committee of people playing the piano."

For Gould, it was as if he had discovered CD 318 all over again—not in terms of its sound, but in the all-important action, which was more to his liking than any he had found in years. It is very possible that Gould, who for his entire career had been playing on the best Steinway had to offer, had never played a Yamaha piano. In fact, he responded in a way that had become familiar to the Yamaha salespeople, who were increasingly witnessing the shocked reaction of many professional pianists upon discovering the evenness of the Yamaha action. Unlike Steinway's, Yamaha's manufacturing process was automated, and while Steinway's parts may have been handmade, in the 1970s the quality had plummeted. Yamaha, through its more automated process, emphasized consistency, especially when it came to the plates and the weight of the keys.

Yamaha's aesthetic approach to its instruments was also different. It rejected the American bravura piano in favor of a more graceful instrument. When Gould played a Yamaha with these basic characteristics that had, in addition, been lovingly regulated and maintained by one of Yamaha's very best technicians, he fell for it immediately and decided to buy it on the spot.

When Edquist heard that Gould had bought a Yamaha and

planned to record the Goldberg Variations on it, he was dumb-founded. Throughout his career as a technician he had chronically disapproved of the mass-produced Yamaha brand. He didn't feel betrayed, exactly; he knew as well as Gould that old 318 was beyond salvation. But couldn't Gould at least have settled on a Steinway?

It wasn't long before executives at Steinway & Sons got wind of Gould's defection. Someone from Steinway must have spotted the Yamaha after it had been moved from Ostrovsky's to the Thirtieth Street recording studio at CBS Records. Just before the recording was to begin, Gould got a call from an alarmed David Rubin at Steinway, inquiring about Gould's piano affiliation. Oh yes, Gould told him, he was using a Yamaha. He had even bought one. But he still considered himself a Steinway artist. There was nothing he would like more than to find a good Steinway, he assured Rubin, and went out of his way to remind him of the unsuccessful trips he had made to New York in search of a piano that was suitable for his recording needs. He told Rubin that the Yamaha had a magnificent action, similar to Steinway CD 318 when it was newer and in better health. But, playing both sides, he told Rubin that the Yamaha was only a "temporary stopgap" until he could find a Steinway that he was happy with.

Gould never did hear about Mitsuo Azuma, the technician who regulated the Yamaha to the glorious state in which he had discovered it behind the sheets on Fifty-sixth Street. Now that it was time for Debbi Ostrovsky to supply Gould with a technician, she sent him a man named Daniel Mansolino, a highly respected technician who had been working at Ostrovsky's on a freelance basis on and off for several years. In contrast to the humble Edquist, Mansolino was a man with an outsized personality who thought highly of his own abilities as a technician. And indeed, he was very talented.

Now, with the Yamaha in CD 318's former role, it was Mansolino, not Edquist, whom Gould engaged to minister to the piano when he recorded the Goldbergs at the Thirtieth Street recording studio in April of 1981. In addition to the CBS producer and his technicians, Bruno Monsaingeon was also present with a film crew. The revisiting of the Goldbergs was to be another in the *Glenn Gould Plays Bach* series. Once Gould arrived at the studio, there was always a good deal of banter before the actual work started, with Gould conducting a contrapuntal social hour, carrying on several animated conversations simultaneously. Then eventually he would say, "Well, I can't put off the moment of truth any longer. Time to soak." And he would disappear for the ritual soaking of his hands.

During the recording sessions, Mansolino and Gould worked together closely. By and large, Gould was very pleased with Mansolino's work. He paid him the ultimate compliment when, after playing a particularly difficult passage, he stopped and said into the microphone that was piped into the control booth: "Dan, I know you didn't get a chance to touch up the tuning for that one. And I don't think I can do it any better than that. But if you can't live with the tuning, I'll do it again." Sometimes it seemed as if Gould wanted to please Mansolino more than Mansolino wanted to please Gould.

Gould's perfect ear was often quicker than Mansolino's, just as it had been with Edquist's, pinpointing the instant a note started to work its way out of tune. "Dan, the E in the treble staff: Is that in tune? And the one an octave lower. It's flat. Am I right?"

And so it went. But as the recording session wore on, Gould's love for the Yamaha began to fade. It just didn't have the range of the glorious CD 318. Monsaingeon's film provides a marvelous running commentary on the Yamaha's shortcomings. Variation 5, with its famous intricacy and devilishly fast tempo, lasted just a little over half a minute, but it was one "where the Yamaha is, frankly, not quite up to it," Gould complained. Variation 14 was similarly problematic. "The problem in this piano is the trilling," he said. "It doesn't do it very well, especially in the center octave, and there's only so much that one can do to distract from that fact." Or this, during a particularly nettlesome passage: "This is a very, very difficult one to do on this piano. It's just not something you can make clear in a machine-gun-like way, as you can on 318."

In that short series of recording sessions, it was as if the years with Edquist during CD 318's heavy tweaking period in the 1960s were condensed into three days with Mansolino. In fact, less time was spent recording and filming than bringing in Mansolino, who continually readjusted the action whenever there was an off note. "He would call in the technician and they would spend hours with the mechanics out of the piano with the technician working on it and Glenn just watching," Monsaingeon recalled.

Gould was constantly remarking on the Yamaha's problems, trying his best to articulate the issues that he wanted Mansolino to fix. "The low E is still a little loud," he would complain. Or: "I don't want to get you into uncharted waters, but at the moment there is a strong sense of the vertical and what I want is a horizontal experience." What he wanted was something "as smooth and as nonexistent as possible." It was an odd request, but understandable in light of what Gould had done on 318 with, say, Orlando Gibbons's music, where the piano's light action had allowed his fingers to skate along the surface of the keys.

After Gould finished a take, it wasn't unusual for him to bend his head as if in prayer, put his hands between his knees, and lean back in the chair. "Thank you, Glenn, I think that's just glorious," came the producer's voice over the speaker. And Gould would answer, "Considering what I'm having to deal with here,

I don't think I can do any better." Finally Gould came up with a way to convey in more tangible terms what he wanted Mansolino to do: "Think harpsichord," he told the technician. "I want a harpsichord. Virtually."

Lorne Tulk, Gould's longtime sound engineer, guessed that Gould was feeling guilty for playing a Yamaha, later observing that "he still felt a loyalty to Steinway, even though he had provoked them in numerous ways in the past." After a while during the recording sessions, Gould resorted to calling the Yamaha "this thing."

Clearly he was missing what he had once been able to do on CD 318. "I can't get it on this piano," he said during one of the rapid-fire variations. "I want it as a machine-gun effect and get it at home routinely, but I can't do it here." Then, as if determined not to mope, he suddenly brightened up. "But we'll try it again!"

The Goldberg sessions continued, and by the time Gould reached Variation 30, for reasons no one could quite understand, the piano began inching its way back into favor: "It's not as good as it had been. It's lost that incredible smoothness. But it's better." In fact, the music Gould created in those recording sessions was remarkable, even thrilling. When the new Goldberg Variations were released in September 1982, the critic Tim Page, a longtime friend and admirer of Gould's who had found the first recording filled with originality, intelligence, and fire, liked the second one even more. He found it more thoughtful—more meditative—and observed that as the pianist advanced into his forties, Gould was "no longer just an arrogant, albeit sweet-tempered, genius. He became a sweet-tempered, melancholy genius."

Other critics, for the most part, agreed. They found the later recording intellectually far more commanding than the earlier one, though not free of some classic showing off on Gould's part: Most of the virtuosic variations still raced at imponderably fast tempos. At the same time, the second time around Gould was more calculated with his phrasing and ornamentation. The pianist David Dubal described the new recording as "a Goldberg infused with humanity." It was as if Gould's spirit as a man and his breadth as a musician had grown and changed since the first time he recorded these pieces. The aria, in particular, had what Dubal called a "terrible, withdrawn pain that is unforgettable." Through the ensuing years, the work would be given even more prominence among the pianist's oeuvre—heard as "autumnal" and as Gould's final "testament." For within a week of the album's release, Gould was dead.

BY THE SUMMER of 1982 Gould's health had begun to deteriorate in earnest. His eyes were perpetually bloodshot, and he always looked tired and haggard. On his lined legal pads, he noted his medical symptoms: palpitations, heat in arm, freezing sensations, "indigestive-style pains in chest." Part of the malaise was surely his hyperactive hypochondriac's imagination. He had once written that he had discovered some odd blue spots on his abdomen, precisely "in the area where the hiatus hernia is often knotted up." As it turned out, they were ink stains from the very ballpoint pen with which he was writing the note. But this time the problems were real.

Gould had often, and famously, proclaimed that when he turned fifty he would stop playing the piano, or at least stop making piano recordings. He said he had run out of music, having recorded virtually all of the piano music that interested him. And he wasn't particularly open to recording music that challenged his own prepossessions as a musician. He had never moved beyond the self-satisfied teenager who dismissed Mozart's concertos. In his darker moments, Gould told friends that he did not think he would live much past fifty. This had been a persistent refrain while he was with Cornelia, who tried to reassure him that his fear was unfounded. Now, despite the fact that his mother had lived to be eighty-three, he worried that the hypertension that killed her would do the same to him. When he turned fifty on September 25, 1982, there were many published tributes, often tied to the release of the Goldberg Variations. Buoyed by the attention, Gould continued to stay busy. He had clearly not made a definitive decision about whether he would in fact stop making new piano recordings, because he was telling friends and colleagues of future plans for recordings he intended to make. He even spoke of moonlighting as a recording producer, having done so once as a favor for a friend in 1973. In the midst of the excitement around the release of the Goldberg Variations and his ideas for what to do next, he was temporarily distracted from the hypertension he had been so focused on; his only health-related complaint around his birthday was a cold, accompanied by sinus pressure that refused to go away.

Two days after his birthday, however, he awoke feeling strange. He had a terrible headache and his left leg was numb. He called Roberts, who came over right away and called the doctor, who, in view of Gould's hypochondriacal tendencies, said he was not terribly worried. But Gould was frightened. He thought he had had a stroke. As the day wore on, he felt worse. His speech began to slur, and his entire left side became paralyzed. Roberts put in several more calls to the doctor, who, upon hearing of the new symptoms, began to take the matter seriously and told Roberts to call an ambulance. Instead, Roberts got Gould down to his car in a wheelchair and drove him to a hospital in downtown Toronto. They arrived shortly after eight P.M. Notes made in the emergency room at the time indicated muscular weakness over the left side of the body and drowsiness, but Gould had no difficulty speaking. The diagnosis in the emergency room was indeed stroke, and he was admitted to the neurology department for further observation. The next day he remained paralyzed on his left side, the headache worsened, and his vision began to deteriorate. He slept a great deal, but he was able to talk and watch television. Friends and family members began gathering at the hospital, and he was able to speak with his father and his favorite cousin, Jessie Greig. But by that night he was confused and disoriented. Moving in and out of consciousness, he became incoherent. He told a nurse he was in a recording studio. As Roberts later recalled, Gould started to ramble and lose control. "I can remember having to leave him. He was getting more and more upset," he said many years later. "I had to leave. I just knew instinctively that I couldn't be there. And I can still hear him calling me." His father found him asleep most of the time, occasionally making conducting movements with his right arm.

By the next evening Gould was comatose and relying on a breathing tube. Once it was clear that he had suffered massive brain damage and was essentially brain-dead, his father made the decision to withdraw life-support systems. On the morning of October 4, Glenn Gould was pronounced dead. An autopsy performed later that day revealed two blood clots, one from sometime in the summer and another that was probably about ten days old, which had likely caused the sinus pressure that Gould had complained about on his birthday.

When Gould died, grief filled the classical airwaves as radio stations devoted extensive programming to his music. Newspapers immediately carried lengthy tributes to the pianist, and shock and sorrow over his premature death spread around the world. Many of his millions of fans took his death as a personal loss. "I write my plays to Glenn Gould," remarked the playwright Tina Howe. "I cook the kids' spaghetti dinners to Glenn

Gould. I pay the bills to Glenn Gould." And something about the sudden death of a relatively young man was difficult for many of his fans, most of whom had never seen him play in public, to accept.

Before the funeral, which was a small, private ceremony, Gould's friends and colleagues paid their respects at a funeral home. The public memorial service was held a week later in Saint Paul's Anglican, the largest church in Toronto. Three thousand people came from around the world. Gould had once remarked that he would have liked to attend his own memorial, to see who showed up. And indeed he was there, playing his own requiem. At the end of the service, the closing aria from the recent recording of the Goldberg Variations was piped into the cathedral. His grave is marked by a simple granite stone into which the outline of a piano is etched, along with his name, years of birth and death, and the first three measures of the same aria.

ELEVEN

Afterlife

A view of CD 318 and its cast-iron plate. The piano is now at the Library and Archives Canada in Ottawa. Photograph by Ian Austen, courtesy of Ian Austen.

By EARLY 1984, EIGHTEEN months after Gould's death, CD 318 had taken up residence under the main stairwell at the National Library of Canada in Ottawa, where it would remain for the next decade. The pygmy chair took its place next to the elevators on the fourth floor, in a Plexiglas display case. Gould's other pianos were scattered around Canada. The smaller Steinway that he had kept at his apartment was completely rebuilt and refurbished before ending up at Rideau Hall, the governor general's house in Ottawa. The Yamaha that Gould used for the final Goldberg recording eventually went to Roy Thomson Hall in Toronto, where it is played regularly to this day. Another Yamaha he bought near the end of his life ended up at a church in Edmonton. The venerable Chickering came to rest on display at the CBC's Glenn Gould Studio in Toronto.

The director of the National Library's music division, Helmut Kallmann, was determined to learn everything he could about the library's new treasure, and so a few months after CD 318 arrived he traveled to Toronto to visit Verne Edquist. The tuner told him the whole story of the piano's life, including the devastating accident at the Eaton's loading dock and the many subsequent attempts to restore the action to its original—and, having forsaken that goal, to just playable—condition. Kallmann asked him to come to Ottawa to tune and regulate the old piano, and Edquist happily agreed. He packed his tools and a small suitcase and took the train to Ottawa.

As part of its agreement to sell the piano to the National Library, the Gould estate had imposed several conditions about its use, the most important being that beyond basic tuning there was to be no modifying of the instrument. But "because of its specially adapted action and mechanism," the estate stipulated,

CD 318 was "to be kept in active and playing order, to be available to researchers and scholars studying the technique of Glenn Gould."

Kallmann appreciated the value of the piano both as a teaching instrument as well as for the virtues that Gould had so prized. In a letter to the estate shortly after CD 318 arrived, he noted that "For ordinary mortals who prefer a light action and an instrument suited for contrapuntal music, the instrument is still a joy to play and listen to." He had no intention of treating the instrument as a museum piece, but rather as a working recital piano, so in accordance with the wishes of the estate as well as his own desire to honor the remarkable piano, he informed his staff that "if a pianist does not like its particular adjustments, we won't change a thing."

WHEN EDQUIST ARRIVED at the library, he found that CD 318, now referred to by the library staff as "the Gould Piano," seemed in good condition, not much worse off than when he had last worked on it a few years earlier. While working on the piano, he found it an odd and eerie experience to be in the presence of the piano without Gould there to play and kibitz about the state of its tuning, or to hatch some new and highly improbable idea for how to optimize its sound or its action.

After Gould had finally declared CD 318 unplayable and had purchased the two Yamahas, Edquist gradually began to focus his professional efforts elsewhere, taking on a variety of private clients. Gould had been known to cut off friendships and professional relationships, sometimes abruptly, when they no longer served a need of some kind. But in this case there had been no definitive parting of the ways. Gould's switch to Yamaha simply meant he didn't need Edquist as much, and they gradually drifted out of each other's orbits. Edquist understood this, yet still he was deeply dismayed that no one had phoned him after Gould's sudden death, and that he had heard the news the way that it had come to so many millions of strangers—on the radio, followed by strains of the aria from the Goldberg Variations.

THE OFFICIAL INAUGURATION of CD 318 in its new home took place on October 14, 1986, in a recital that featured Angela Hewitt, a young Canadian who had recently won a Bach competition held in Gould's memory. Hewitt was a rising star who had started playing Bach at the age of four and conquered the Goldberg Variations at sixteen. By 2005 she would finish an eleven-year project to record all the major keyboard works of Bach, which won her a huge following. Critics over the years would hail her as "the preeminent Bach pianist of our time" and "nothing less than the pianist who will define Bach performance on the piano for years to come."

Hewitt had grown up listening to Gould's records, and had seen him regularly on Canadian television. She remembers telling her parents when she was a small child that he seemed to her "a kook," with his nose practically on the keyboard, playing at tempos that even at a young age she knew were bizarre. "He was clearly recognizable as a serious presence in Canadian musical life, but not, perhaps, one to be closely imitated," she observed. More importantly, "he set this wonderful standard of Bach playing and brought it to such a large audience that I admire him for that." For the library debut of CD 318, Hewitt was deferential in her choice of music: She played Bach—one of the French Suites—and a Weber sonata. And for her encore, of course, she played the aria from the Goldberg Variations.

Recitals on CD 318 have continued through the years. Eventually it was moved to the library auditorium and a harpsichord took its place under the stairwell. It even made the local news when, in the middle of a performance, one key suddenly stopped working. Some musicians were even permitted to record on CD 318, including a classically trained pianist named Ian Hepburn who had made his career in rock 'n' roll. The famous hiccup was still very much a presence when Hepburn played 318, and it still bedeviled the sound engineers. A string of jazz pianists played the piano, and as soon as they touched the keys, they sensed Gould's aura. Said one: "I sat down to play Monk and out came Bach."

In the early 1990s, CD 318 landed a film role and was sent to Toronto for the shooting of *Thirty-two Short Films About Glenn Gould*, an idiosyncratic homage to the pianist. The instrument appears throughout the film, and one segment, three and a half minutes long, is devoted to 318 itself. A celebration of the interior topography of the piano, the segment abandons the customary focus on a pianist's hands to reveal the intricacy of the mechanism, the actual beauty of 318 under its lid. In one sensuous sequence, as Gould is heard playing his harpsichordistic rendition of the Bach Prelude and Fugue in C Minor from book one of the *Well-Tempered Clavier*, the camera seems to inhabit the interior of 318. Gliding gracefully over the golden plate, it pans across the furrowed landscape of the strings, then shifts to a close-up of the hammers doing their rhythmic dance.

Edquist was brought in for the making of the film, both as an interviewee and to tend to the piano while it was being used. When the filmmakers asked if they might remove the plate brace to get the camera still closer, the ever-protective tuner declined. Years later he observed that it was during the shooting of that film that the reality of Gould's absence finally sank in. And although he was a fundamentally practical man, not inclined to believe in the supernatural, throughout the making of the film Edquist got a strong, unmistakable sense of Gould's spirit around the piano.

One of the film's final scenes showed the 1977 launch of the *Voyager I* spacecraft, which carried with it a golden record assembled by a NASA committee chaired by the astronomer Carl Sagan. The record included 115 images, greetings in fifty-five languages, and the sounds of surf, thunder, whale song, children singing, a human kiss, and a mother greeting her newborn. This bottle that had been launched "into the cosmic ocean," as Sagan described it, also included musical selections from different cultures and eras that epitomized human achievement. One of these was the music of Johann Sebastian Bach, played by Glenn Gould on his favorite piano. It was the Prelude and Fugue in C, which Gould had recorded in the 1960s at Eaton Auditorium on CD 318 when the piano was at its very best. "When I heard that," Edquist said, "it was like a dream. There's Bach writing the music, Glenn is playing the music, and it's my tuning that's giving it voice. And it's going somewhere in outer space."

Well into the piano's new life, a Hungarian-born pianist named Mary Kenedi was invited to give a recital at the library. She chose a lively program of Liszt, Kodály, and Bartók. Gould had not been a particular fan of any of these men: He once called Bartók one of the most overestimated of modern composers, and he was equally dismissive of Liszt, who represented all that he hated about piano virtuosity, showmanship, and Dionysian hedonism. Of Kodály he made no acknowledgment whatsoever.

Kenedi, however, was completely devoted to the works of Hungarian composers, and she had chosen an all-Hungarian program for this recital, which was being held in honor of the Hungarian ambassador to Canada, who had personally asked her to perform. The pianist had selected her pieces with care. She had fallen in love with the Liszt piece *Les Jeux d'Eau à la Villa d'Este* while studying in Budapest, and it presented a series of technical challenges that Kenedi had long since mastered. She had been a friend to Béla Bartók, who often played Kodály's *Transylvanian Lament* in his recitals, so she included that selection in the program along with several other Kodály pieces. But Bartók was her true love, and so she chose his music to end the program: a handful of early pieces, as well as some of the famous works from *Fifteen Hungarian Peasant Songs*. These pieces, which Bartók had based on folk songs and which were infused with national flavor, color, and expression, would enable Kenedi to unleash her own romantic and fiery temperament.

Kenedi was particularly honored to be there. She had once played on one of Horowitz's favorite pianos, and had been thrilled to touch Bartók's own Bösendorfer. Now here she was, in one of Canada's most august institutions, playing Glenn Gould's beloved Steinway.

She had rehearsed on 318 the afternoon before the concert and immediately appreciated the piano's tonal richness, which allowed her to paint colors, especially in the Bartók. But she was put off by the action. The keys moved much too easily. "The scary experience was that I like to play on a piano that has resistance, and it didn't have any." The faster she played, the harder she found it. Keys were flying as if on their own. Afterward, Kenedi asked the tuner who was standing by if he could help. He replied that he wasn't allowed to do anything more than tune the piano, and most certainly he could not tamper with the action.

Undaunted, Kenedi began her performance that evening with the Liszt, the most sedate piece on the hour-long program. Then she worked her way up through the Kodály. Kenedi was a vigorous pianist, and before long her zeal for the music had begun to assert itself. By the time she reached Bartók's rousing *Folk Dances*, she noticed that something odd was happening: The piano was beginning to inch away from her.

Apparently someone had forgotten to set the wheels to keep the piano in place. As the piano crept toward the edge of the stage, Kenedi began to fear that it might end up in the laps of the people in the front row. The first thing she did was try to restrain her playing. But the piano kept moving. Then she tried to actually pull the piano back toward her, but she couldn't without lifting her hands from the keyboard. Even between pieces she could gain no purchase under the keys. And it would have been unseemly, to say the least, to have gotten down on her knees and clutched at the legs. So she resorted to her only remaining option: She slid her chair closer to the keyboard, inching it forward as the piano edged away from the forceful playing. The piano, apparently in full retreat from Kenedi's un-Gouldian repertoire, was moving in a general westerly direction, toward Toronto. By now the pianist was not only distracted by the moving piano, but she was trying to read the audience to see if anyone else had noticed. Luckily it seemed that no one had, and she kept playing.

By the end of the concert, Kenedi, the bench, and the piano had traveled at least a foot from their original spot on the stage. The applause was loud, appreciative, and sustained. As Kenedi rose from her seat she bowed, then smiled and shot CD 318 a sidelong glance. "Where?" she asked the piano silently. "Where were you trying to go?"

Acknowledgments

In the fall of 2002, I attended the Sonatas, a piano camp in Vermont, where for ten days I was surrounded by pianos of all sizes and by people who simply love the instrument. It was after that trip that I decided the story of one piano might make an interesting book. I am grateful to Polly van der Linde, the director of the camp and a great pianist and teacher, for her initial enthusiasm for the idea. Fellow camper Keith Pinter, recounting a scene from *Thirty-two Short Films About Glenn Gould* over dinner one night, planted the Glenn Gould seed in my head. Other Sonatans, notably Michele Bernstein, John Kelley, Beth McGilvray, Ed Ewing, and Nova Fraser, inspired me along the way.

I am deeply indebted to the staff at the Library and Archives Canada, particularly Cheryl Gillard and Gilles St-Laurent, not only for their assistance while I was in Ottawa in 2004, but for their subsequent help and encouragement from afar. Gilles St-Laurent arranged the reunion of the piano and the chair for the photograph on the cover, taken by my *New York Times* colleague Ian Austen.

I am grateful to Susan Hawkshaw and Vivian Perlis at Yale University's Oral History, American Music collection for access to their Steinway Project archives. Thanks, too, to Richard Lieberman and Douglas Di Carlo at the La Guardia and Wagner

Archives at La Guardia Community College, CUNY, for access to oral histories there. At the Ontario Archives in Toronto, where the archives of T. Eaton Co. reside, staff members, especially Barb Taylor, were helpful and quick.

Malcolm Lester and Stephen Posen of the Glenn Gould Estate were accommodating and encouraging, as were Brian Levine and Faye Perkins of the Glenn Gould Foundation. I am grateful to the estate for permission to quote from Gould's letters and diaries.

Many thanks to Lorne Tulk, Verne Edquist, Ted Sambell, Henry Z. Steinway, Raphael Mostel, Robert Silverman, Cornelia Foss, Bruno Monsaingeon, Helmut Kallmann, Franz Mohr, Ray Roberts, Mary Kenedi, John Roberts, Tim Maloney, Ian Hepburn, Gary Graffman, and Noami Graffman for their recollections.

For help with research questions large and small, I am grateful to Roy Kehl, Anne Acker, Tali Mahanor, Ian Austen, Gretchen Roberts, Tim Page, Kevin Fryer, James Barron, Lisa Crawford, Carol Montparker, Richard Lieberman, Kieran Clifford, and Sergei Riabtchenko.

Early readers included Susie Zacharias, Hank Long, Denny Lyon, Miles Graber, John Callahan, Susan Crawford, Amy Slater, Kathy Loram, Brad Johnson, Bruce Headlam, Kevin Bazzana, Christopher Ris, Marilynn Rowland, and David Rowland.

Thanks to Zoë Lyon—my shining light of a daughter—for her patience and willingness to put up with her mother's periodic journeys into writerly seclusion.

Kevin Bazzana is a gentleman and a scholar if ever there was one. He was generous far beyond the call, with his time, his encyclopedic knowledge of all things Gouldian, and his cheerful willingness to read my "weird little book" over and over. A sit-down comedian of the first order, his replies to my every query weren't merely exhaustive and authoritative, but often filled with hilarious asides. Many thanks to him and Sharon Bristow for the dinners, hospitality, and *The Simpsons Movie* in Brentwood Bay, B.C.

John Callahan, an expert piano technician and a specialist in the restoration of Steinway pianos in the San Francisco Bay area, painstakingly read the manuscript for technical accuracy through at least a half-dozen iterations. With each reading, he told me, he sympathized more and more with Gould's frustration over the repairs done to CD 318, and it grew increasingly clear to him that if Glenn Gould had been working in today's world of high-end piano restoration and custom action balancing, the piano's fate would probably have turned out very differently.

Kathy Loram read the manuscript in its infancy and was encouraging when there wasn't much to be encouraging about. Not only was she my most inspiring muse in the book's formative stages, but she was an enthusiastic, careful listener and a still more careful reader. I cannot thank her enough for her intellectual generosity.

Marilynn Rowland, my gifted piano teacher, started me on this path toward piano passion. Steven Levy encouraged me to write about something I truly cared about. Katinka Matson, my longtime agent, championed the book from the start. Daniel Preysman conducted crucial early interviews. Michael Hawley was another early cheerleader.

Annik LaFarge, my editor at Bloomsbury USA, rescued this book from an uncertain fate. Annik is the best thing that has ever happened to me as a writer. She knew exactly what to do at every turn and let nothing slip past her. She possesses the uncanny ability to make a writer want to work her hardest, pushing ever so gently, but pushing all the same. Annik's assistant, Benjamin Adams, was always helpful. Will Georgantas copyedited the manuscript with a keen and learned eye. Thanks, too, to Greg Villepique,

Gillian Blake, Peter Miller, Jason Bennett, and Amy King at Bloomsbury USA and to Doug Pepper, Jenny Bradshaw, and Adria Iwasutiak at McClelland & Stewart in Toronto.

From the start, Brad Johnson was not only a loving spouse but an exacting editor, supportive sounding board, and brilliant wordsmith. Over the course of four years, he accompanied me from coast to coast in Canada, cheered me along, and cheered me up—and made no fewer than a thousand perfect cups of coffee. I could not have asked for a more wonderful partner while writing a book. It is with deep appreciation that I am dedicating this book to him and to my amazing mother, Susie Zacharias, who called early and often to offer her support and her love.

Bibliography

Barclay, Robert. *Preservation and Use of Historic Musical Instruments: Display Case or Concert Hall.* London: Earthscan Publications Ltd., 2004.

Barron, James. *Piano: The Making of a Steinway Concert Grand.* New York: Times Books, 2006.

Bazzana, Kevin. *Glenn Gould: The Performer in the Work.* Oxford: Clarendon Press, 1997.

———. *Wondrous Strange: The Life and Art of Glenn Gould.* New York: Oxford University Press, 2004.

Beckwith, John. "Glenn Gould, the Early Years: Addenda and Corrigenda." *GlennGould* (Fall 1996).

———. *In Search of Alberto Guerrero.* Waterloo, ON: Wilfrid Laurier University Press, 2006.

Bergman, Rhona. *The Idea of Gould.* Philadelphia: Lev Publishing, 1999.

Bliven Junior, Bruce. "Piano Man." *The New Yorker* (May 9, 1953).

Carhart, Thad. *The Piano Shop on the Left Bank: The Hidden World of a Paris Atelier.* London: Chatto & Windus, 2000.

Chasins, Abram. *Speaking of Pianists . . .* New York: Alfred A. Knopf, 1957.

"Concert Not-So-Grands." *Time* (September 3, 1973).

Cott, Jonathan. *Conversations with Glenn Gould.* Boston: Little, Brown, 1984.

Dubal, David. *The Art of the Piano: Its Performers, Literature and Recordings.* Pompton Plains, NJ: Amadeus Press, 2004.

———. *Reflections from the Keyboard: The World of the Concert Pianist.* New York: Schirmer Books, 1997.

Dudley, Ray. "Alberto Guerrero and Glenn Gould: My View." *New Journal for Music* (Summer 1990).

Edquist, Verne, ed. *Centre Walk: Former Students of the Ontario School for the Blind Recall School Memories.* Toronto: Phillips Publishers Ltd., 1993.

Fostle, Don W. *The Steinway Saga: An American Dynasty.* New York: Scribner, 1995.

Friedrich, Otto. *Glenn Gould: A Life and Variations.* New York: Random House, 1989.

Fries, Emil B. *But You Can Feel It.* Portland, OR: Binford & Mort, 1980.

Glenn Gould Extasis, CBC Home Video, 1993.

Glenn Gould Hereafter. Directed by Bruno Monsaingeon. Ideale Audience International, 2006.

Glenn Gould Life & Times. CBC Home Video, 1998.

Glenn Gould: The Alchemist. Directed by Bruno Monsaingeon. Ideale Audience International, 2002.

Gould, Glenn. "Stokowski in Six Scenes." *Piano Quarterly* (Winter 1977–Summer 1978).

Graffman, Gary. *I Really Should Be Practicing.* New York: Doubleday, 1981.

Gray, James H. *The Winter Years: The Depression on the Prairies.* Toronto: Macmillan of Canada, 1966.

Green, Gill. "History of Piano Tuning." UK Piano Pages (www.uk-piano.org/history/piano-tuner-history.html).

Hamilton, Kenneth. *After the Golden Age: Romantic Pianism and Modern Performance.* New York: Oxford University Press, 2008.

Johnson, David. "Bach's Keyboard Partitas: A Conversation with Glenn Gould." *GlennGould* (Fall 1998). Original interview 1963.

Kazdin, Andrew. *Glenn Gould at Work: Creative Lying.* New York: E. P. Dutton, 1989.

Lenehan, Michael. "Building the Steinway Grand Piano K2571: The Quality of the Instrument." *The Atlantic Monthly* (August 1982).

Lieberman, Richard K. *Steinway & Sons.* New Haven: Yale University Press, 1997.

Loesser, Arthur. *Men, Women and Pianos: A Social History.* Mineola, NY: Dover Publications, 1991.

Lott, R. Allen. *From Paris to Peoria: How European Piano Virtuosos Brought Classical Music to the American Heartland.* New York: Oxford University Press, 2003.

Mach, Elyse. *Great Pianists Speak for Themselves.* London: Robson Books, 1981.

Maxwell, Joan, and Harvey Rempel. "The Glenn We Knew." *GlennGould* (Fall 2007).

McClure, John. "Glenn Gould: Concert Dropout." *GlennGould* (Fall 2001); Columbia/CBS Masterworks LP, 1984.

McGreevey, John, ed. *Glenn Gould: Variations.* Toronto: Macmillan of Canada, 1983.

Mohr, Franz, and Edith Schaeffer. *My Life with the Great Pianists.* Grand Rapids, MI: Baker Book House, 1992.

Montparker, Carol. *The Anatomy of a New York Debut Recital: A Chronicle.* Evanston, IL: The Instrumentalist Company, 1984.

Ostwald, Peter. *Glenn Gould: The Ecstasy and Tragedy of Genius.* New York: W. W. Norton, 1997.

Page, Tim. "On Bach's Goldberg Variations: Glenn Gould in Conversation with Tim Page." *GlennGould* (Spring 2001); *Glenn Gould: A State of Wonder.* Sony Classical compact disc, 2002.

Page, Tim, ed. *The Glenn Gould Reader.* New York: Vintage, 1990.

Parakilas, James. *Piano Roles: A New History of the Piano.* New Haven: Yale University Press, 2002.

Payzant, Geoffrey. *Glenn Gould, Music and Mind.* Toronto: Key Porter Books, 1984.

Ratcliffe, Ronald V. *Steinway.* San Francisco: Chronicle Books, 1989.

Roberts, John L. *The Art of Glenn Gould: Reflections of a Musical Genius.* Toronto: Malcolm Lester Books, 1999.

Roberts, John L., and Ghyslaine Guertin, eds. *Glenn Gould: Selected Letters.* New York: Oxford University Press, 1992.

Roddy, Joseph. "Apollonian." *The New Yorker* (May 14, 1960).

Roell, Craig H. *The Piano in America, 1890–1940*. Chapel Hill: The University of North Carolina Press, 1989.

Santink, Joy L. *Timothy Eaton and the Rise of His Department Store*. Toronto: University of Toronto Press, 1990.

Schonberg, Harold. *The Great Pianists: From Mozart to the Present*. New York: Simon & Schuster, 1987.

Steinway & Sons. Official Web site (www.steinway.com).

Taylor, David. "Paderewski's Piano." *Smithsonian* (March 1999).

"The Goldberg Variations," *Glenn Gould Plays Bach*. Directed by Bruno Monsaingeon. Sony Classical, 2000.

Tovell, Vincent. "At Home with Glenn Gould." The Glenn Gould Foundation compact disc, 1996.

Primary Sources and Oral Histories

The most important collection of primary-source material related to Glenn Gould and CD 318 resides in the Glenn Gould Archive, archival fond MUS 109 in the Music Division of the Library and Archives Canada in Ottawa. The archive maintains an exhaustive and highly searchable online database (www.collectionscanada.gc.ca/glenn gould/), which pointed me to all mentions of CD 318 in the archive. In Ottawa, I followed up on those leads and perused thousands of Gould's letters, notepads, and diaries; there I also viewed outtakes from the 1981 Goldberg Variations sessions and listened to several tape recordings of Gould trying out different pianos. Permission to quote from Gould's correspondence and journals comes from the Glenn Gould Estate.

Interviews with Henry Z. Steinway were conducted in person and by telephone. I also used an interview he gave to the Yale University Oral History, American Music project in 1978. From that collection, called the Steinway Project, I also consulted interviews conducted with William Hupfer, Rosalyn Tureck, Winston Fitzgerald, Gary Graffman, David Rubin, and Franz Mohr.

Another rich and important trove of oral histories resides in the Steinway Collection at the LaGuardia and Wagner Archives at La-Guardia Community College, CUNY. Several of the people interviewed were workers in the Steinway factory in the 1940s, when CD 318 was being built. The interviews consulted from that collection include those with Walter Drasche and Joe and Ralph Bisceglie.

Information about the completion and distribution of pianos built just before and just after CD 318 was provided by Roy Kehl and Tali Mahanor.

Notes

1. Toronto

For biographical material relating to Gould, I relied heavily on Kevin Bazzana's exhaustive and definitive Gould biography, *Wondrous Strange: The Life and Art of Glenn Gould.*

11   *took him to see Walt Disney's*   Tim Page, ed., *The Glenn Gould Reader* (New York: Vintage, 1990), 261.

11   *A childhood nanny*   Kevin Bazzana, *Wondrous Strange: The Life and Art of Glenn Gould* (New York: Oxford University Press, 2004), 335.

12   *The piano became the place where Glenn preferred*   Peter Ostwald, *Glenn Gould: The Ecstasy and Tragedy of Genius* (New York: W. W. Norton, 1997), 47.

12   *took him to the Toronto Symphony*   Vincent Tovell, "At Home with Glenn Gould" (Glenn Gould Foundation compact disc, 1996).

12   *Elizabeth Fox, a friend and frequent visitor*   Otto Friedrich, *Glenn Gould: A Life and Variations* (New York: Random House, 1989), 23.

13   *Throughout his life Gould would vehemently*   Bazzana, *Wondrous Strange*, 79.

13   *In general, his father recalled*   Bazzana, *Wondrous Strange*, 32.

16   *Although later in life Gould seldom cited*   John Beckwith, *In Search of Alberto Guerrero* (Waterloo, ON: Wilfrid Laurier University Press, 2006), 4.

16 *Guerrero developed some early habits* John Beckwith, "Glenn, Gould, The Early Years: Addenda and Corrigenda," *GlennGould* (Fall 1996): 57–61.

17 *Wrote Beckwith, "It accounts"* Beckwith, *In Search*, 102.

17 *In an interview he gave much later* John Roberts, *The Art of Glenn Gould: Reflections of a Musical Genius* (Toronto: Malcolm Lester Books, 1999), 260–61.

19 *Gary Graffman and Eugene Istomin, both rising stars* David Dubal, *Reflections from the Keyboard: The World of the Concert Pianist* (New York: Schirmer Books, 1997), 191.

21 *"exactly the right contour"* Roberts, *The Art of Glenn Gould*, 42.

21 *Bach wrote the Goldberg Variations* Joseph Roddy, transcript from 1981 interview.

23 *When discussing his technique* Andrew Kazdin, *Glenn Gould at Work: Creative Lying* (New York: E. P. Dutton, 1989), 103.

24 *She once colorfully described* Elyse Mach, *Great Contemporary Pianists Speak for Themselves* (London: Robson Books, 1981), 165.

25 *By 1960, it had sold forty thousand* Joseph Roddy, "Appolonian," *The New Yorker* (May 14, 1960): 52.

27 *A woman once sent a letter to Columbia Records* Kazdin, *Glenn Gould at Work*, 109.

27 *During one of the first recording sessions* Bazzana, *Wondrous Strange*, 248.

2. Saskatchewan

The bulk of the material on Verne Edquist, his childhood in Saskatchewan, the years spent at the Ontario School for the Blind, and his training and apprenticeship as a piano tuner was derived from a series of interviews I conducted with Edquist between October 2003 and December 2007.

38 *The first blind piano tuner is thought* Gill Green, "History of Piano Tuning," The UK Piano Pages (www.uk-piano.org/history/piano-tuner-history.html).

43 *In the early 1900s, when men* Ibid.

3. Astoria

The three principal texts used for the history of Steinway & Sons were Richard K. Lieberman, *Steinway & Sons* (New Haven: Yale University Press, 1997); Don W. Fostle, *The Steinway Saga* (New York: Scribner, 1995); and Ronald V. Ratcliffe, *Steinway* (San Francisco: Chronicle Books, 1989). The particulars surrounding the building of a Steinway concert grand are drawn in part from Michael Lenehan's fascinating article "Building the Steinway Grand Piano K2571: The Quality of the Instrument," *The Atlantic Monthly* (August 1982).

63   *Upon learning that a Steinway piano*   James Parakilas, *Piano Roles: A New History of the Piano* (New Haven: Yale University Press, 2002), 57.

71   *W 905's soundboard was made*   James Barron, *Piano: The Making of a Steinway Concert Grand* (New York: Times Books, 2006), 79.

73   *Steinway didn't invent the piano action*   Ibid., 94.

4. The Trouble with Pianos

To capture the nature and tone of the relationship between Glenn Gould and Steinway & Sons in the 1950s, I consulted the correspondence between Gould and executives at Steinway & Sons, as well as internal memoranda from the company, all of which are preserved in the Glenn Gould archive at the Library and Archives Canada in Ottawa. For the description of the incident involving William Hupfer, I consulted the Steinway & Sons internal file, which is also now at the Library and Archives Canada.

85   *On one occasion, a hotel piano was*   Alexander Greiner, unpublished memoir, 1957, 107. Cited in Richard K. Lieberman, *Steinway & Sons* (New Haven: Yale University Press, 1997), 183.

85   *David Rubin, a vice president*   Interview with David Rubin, Yale University Steinway Project.

89   *By then, piano manufacturers like Steinway*   Arthur Loesser, *Men, Women and Pianos: A Social History* (Mineola, NY: Dover Publications, 1991), 369.

91   *It was not Beethoven, Mozart, or Chopin*   Bazzana, *Wondrous Strange*, 64.

91 *"You know, the piano is not an instrument"*   David Johnson, "Bach's Keyboard Partitas: A Conversation with Glenn Gould," *GlennGould* (Fall 1998): 53.

91 *If Gould idolized anyone, it was Artur Schnabel*   Bazzana, *Wondrous Strange*, 98.

92 *Graffman was enchanted by CD 199*   Gary Graffman, *I Really Should Be Practicing* (New York: Doubleday, 1981), 188.

93 *CD 15, long a regular*   Bruce Bliven Junior, "Piano Man," *The New Yorker* (May 9, 1953): 44.

94 *Gould was convinced that he needed wider gaps*   Roddy, "Apollonian," 62.

97 *In an 1892 tour, Ignacy Jan Paderewski*   Kenneth Hamilton, *After the Golden Age: Romantic Pianism and Modern Performance* (New York: Oxford University Press, 2008), 135.

99 *In early 1957, Steinway & Sons got a respite*   Bazzana, *Wondrous Strange*, 163–72.

102 *In the 1870s, a pianist named S. B. Mills*   Loesser, *Men, Women and Pianos*, 535.

103 *Hupfer was a stocky, square-jawed*   Bliven, "Piano Man," 56.

105 *Over the years, Gould's fear of germs*   Dubal, *Reflections*, 64.

5. Eaton's

Much of the historical information about the T. Eaton Company, its piano department, and the history of Eaton Auditorium, including concert programs and correspondence regarding the piano department, was found at the Archives of Ontario in Toronto, home to the historical archives of T. Eaton Co. For descriptions of the 1940s, 1950s, and 1960s at Eaton's piano department, I also relied on interviews with George Cook and Verne Edquist.

125 *When I haven't played for a few weeks*   Roberts, *The Art of Glenn Gould*, 269.

126 *Such was the case in Israel*   Jonathan Cott, *Conversations with Glenn Gould* (Boston: Little, Brown, 1984), 33.

6. A Romance on Three Legs

131 *When Edquist arrived at Gould's penthouse*   Verne Edquist, "In Pursuit of Harmony," unpublished essay.

137 *Gould was usually generous*   Bazzana, *Wondrous Strange*, 101.

137 *Horowitz returned Gould's disdain*   Ibid., 255.

138 *But he admired the gentleness and restraint*   Ibid., 220.

142 *Other pianists believed they understood*   Dubal, *Reflections*, 265.

142 *Gould once tried to convince Stephen*   Ibid., 72.

144 *One friend who visited him for lunch*   Joan Maxwell and Harvey Rempel, "The Glenn We Knew," *GlennGould* (Fall 2007): 79.

150 *By the late 1960s, the hair-trigger action*   Glenn Gould and John McClure, "Glenn Gould, Concert Dropout," *GlennGould* (Fall 2001): 47–60.

7. CD 318 in the Studio

The descriptions of late-night recording sessions at Eaton Auditorium were derived from interviews with Verne Edquist and Lorne Tulk, and from Kazdin's *Glenn Gould at Work*.

154 *Carol Montparker agreed*   Carol Montparker, *The Anatomy of a New York Debut Recital: A Chronicle* (Evanston, IL: The Instrumentalist Company, 1984), 49.

154 *Gould's Bach recordings in particular*   Harold Schonberg, *The Great Pianists: From Mozart to the Present* (New York, Simon & Schuster, 1987), 481.

155 *When Gould was around 318, he guarded the piano*   Dubal, *Reflections*, 64.

156 *A German immigrant who had served*   Franz Mohr, *My Life*, 163.

156 *Gould admired Mohr not only because*   Roberts, *The Art of Glenn Gould*, 265.

156 *Mohr tried to make a believer out of Arthur Rubinstein*   Mohr, *My Life*, 56.

158 *At first Gould complained about the sound*   Kazdin, *Glenn Gould at Work*, 40.

9. Making Do

The description of the trip Gould and Ray Roberts took to New York with CD 318's action in the car comes mostly from a private chronicle Gould kept of the trip and an interview with Ray Roberts, conducted in Toronto by Daniel Preysman in 2004. The section on Wittmayer harpsichords was put together with help from Kevin Fryer of Kevin Fryer Harpsichords in San Francisco.

194 *Mohr had spent enough time working on CD 318*   Mohr, *My Life*, 81.

196 *This period was especially hard*   "Concert Not-So-Grands," *Time* (September 3, 1973).

196 *When Ruth Laredo encountered a lousy*   Dubal, *Reflections*, 243.

199 *The end of the relationship with Cornelia*   Ostwald, *Glenn Gould: The Ecstasy and Tragedy*, 291.

201 *In May 1979*   Kazdin, *Glenn Gould at Work*, 149.

10. The Defection

The section on Gould's stroke and subsequent death relied on descriptions provided in Kevin Bazzana, *Wondrous Strange*; Peter Ostwald, *Glenn Gould: The Ecstasy and Tragedy of Genius*; and Otto Friedrich, *Glenn Gould: A Life and Variations*. The description of the 1981 Goldberg sessions comes from documents and videotapes at the National Library, as well as from an interview with Daniel Mansolino conducted by Junichi Miyazawa.

209 *He wanted to record a cohesive interpretation*   Tim Page, "On Bach's Goldberg Variations: Glenn Gould in Conversation with Tim Page," *GlennGould* (Spring 2001): 15.

210 *When Franz Mohr heard that Gould was looking for a piano*   Personal interview with Franz Mohr, summer 2003.

220 *The pianist David Dubal*   David Dubal, *The Art of the Piano: Its Performers, Literature and Recordings* (Pompton Plains, NJ: Amadeus Press, 2004), 140.

220 *By the summer of 1982*   Bazzana, *Wondrous Strange*, 484.

222 *"I write my plays to Glenn Gould"*   Dubal, *The Art of the Piano*, 139.

11. Afterlife

The material for descriptions of CD 318's life at the National Library of Canada and recitals performed on the piano there comes from letters, internal memoranda, and notes preserved in the Glenn Gould Archive.

Index

Note: Page numbers in *italic* refer to photographs.

A Note on the Author

Katie Hafner is a correspondent for the *New York Times*. Before joining the *Times* in 1998 she worked at *Newsweek* and *Business Week*. She is the author of four previous books: *Cyberpunk: Outlaws and Hackers on the Computer Frontier* (with John Markoff); *Where Wizards Stay Up Late: The Origins of the Internet* (with Matthew Lyon); *The Well: A Story of Love, Death and Real Life in the Seminal Online Community*; and *The House at the Bridge: A Story of Modern Germany*. She lives in the San Francisco Bay Area.